MASTER THE™ DSST®

Art of the Western World Exam

About Peterson's®

Peterson's has been your trusted educational publisher for over 50 years. It's a milestone we're quite proud of, as we continue to offer the most accurate, dependable, high-quality educational content in the field, providing you with everything you need to succeed. No matter where you are on your academic or professional path, you can rely on Peterson's for its books, online information, expert test-prep tools, the most up-to-date education exploration data, and the highest quality career success resources—everything you need to achieve your education goals. For our complete line of products, visit **www.petersons.com.**

For more information, contact Peterson's, 4380 S. Syracuse St., Suite 200, Denver, CO 80237; 800-338-3282 Ext. 54229; or visit us online at **www.petersons.com**.

ISBN-13: 978-0-7689-4438-9

Printed in the United States of America

10 9 8 7 6 5 4 3 2 1   22 21 20

Contents

Before You Begin

HOW THIS BOOK IS ORGANIZED

Peterson's *Master the*™ *DSST*® *Art of the Western World Exam* provides a diagnostic test, subject-matter review, and a post-test.

- **Diagnostic Test**—Twenty multiple-choice questions, followed by an answer key with detailed answer explanations
- **Assessment Grid**—A chart designed to help you identify areas that you need to focus on based on your test results
- **Subject-Matter Review**—General overview of the exam subject, followed by a review of the relevant topics and terminology covered on the exam
- **Post-test**—Sixty multiple-choice questions, followed by an answer key and detailed answer explanations

The purpose of the diagnostic test is to help you figure out what you know—or don't know. The twenty multiple-choice questions are similar to the ones found on the DSST exam, and they should provide you with a good idea of what to expect. Once you take the diagnostic test, check your answers to see how you did. Included with each correct answer is a brief explanation regarding why a specific answer is correct, and in many cases, why other options are incorrect. Use the assessment grid to identify the questions you miss so that you can spend more time reviewing that information later. As with any exam, knowing your weak spots greatly improves your chances of success.

Following the diagnostic test is a subject-matter review. The review summarizes the various topics covered on the DSST exam. Key terms are defined; important concepts are explained; and when appropriate, examples are provided. As you read the review, some of the information may seem familiar while other information may seem foreign. Again, take note of the unfamiliar because that will most likely cause you problems on the actual exam.

After studying the subject-matter review, you should be ready for the post-test. The post-test contains sixty multiple-choice items, and it will serve as a dry run for the real DSST exam. There are complete answer explanations at the end of the test.

OTHER DSST® PRODUCTS BY PETERSON'S

Books, flashcards, practice tests, and videos available online at
www.petersons.com/testprep/dsst

- A History of the Vietnam War
- Art of the Western World
- Astronomy
- Business Mathematics
- Business Ethics and Society
- Civil War and Reconstruction
- Computing and Information Technology
- Criminal Justice
- Environmental Science
- Ethics in America
- Ethics in Technology
- Foundations of Education
- Fundamentals of College Algebra
- Fundamentals of Counseling
- Fundamentals of Cybersecurity
- General Anthropology
- Health and Human Development
- History of the Soviet Union
- Human Resource Management

- Introduction to Business
- Introduction to Geography
- Introduction to Geology
- Introduction to Law Enforcement
- Introduction to World Religions
- Lifespan Developmental Psychology
- Math for Liberal Arts
- Management Information Systems
- Money and Banking
- Organizational Behavior
- Personal Finance
- Principles of Advanced English Composition
- Principles of Finance
- Principles of Public Speaking
- Principles of Statistics
- Principles of Supervision
- Substance Abuse
- Technical Writing

Chapter 1

All About the DSST® Exam

WHAT IS DSST®?

Previously known as the DANTES Subject Standardized Tests, the DSST program provides the opportunity for individuals to earn college credit for what they have learned outside of the traditional classroom. Accepted or administered at more than 1,900 colleges and universities nationwide and approved by the American Council on Education (ACE), the DSST program enables individuals to use the knowledge they have acquired outside the classroom to accomplish their educational and professional goals.

WHY TAKE A DSST® EXAM?

DSST exams offer a way for you to save both time and money in your quest for a college education. Why enroll in a college course in a subject you already understand? For more than 30 years, the DSST program has offered the perfect solution for individuals who are knowledgeable in a specific subject and want to save both time and money. A passing score on a DSST exam provides physical evidence to universities of proficiency in a specific subject. More than 1,900 accredited and respected colleges and universities across the nation award undergraduate credit for passing scores on DSST exams. With the DSST program, individuals can shave months off the time it takes to earn a degree.

The DSST program offers numerous advantages for individuals in all stages of their educational development:
- Adult learners
- College students
- Military personnel

Adult learners desiring college degrees face unique circumstances—demanding work schedules, family responsibilities, and tight budgets. Yet adult learners also have years of valuable work experience that can frequently be applied toward a degree through the DSST program. For example, adult learners with on-the-job experience in business and management might be able to skip the Business 101 courses if they earn passing marks on DSST exams such as Introduction to Business and Principles of Supervision.

Adult learners can put their prior learning into action and move forward with more advanced course work. Adults who have never enrolled in a college course may feel a little uncertain about their abilities. If this describes your situation, then sign up for a DSST exam and see how you do. A passing score may be the boost you need to realize your dream of earning a degree. With family and work commitments, adult learners often feel they lack the time to attend college. The DSST program provides adult learners with the unique opportunity to work toward college degrees without the time constraints of semester-long course work. DSST exams take two hours or less to complete. In one weekend, you could earn credit for multiple college courses.

The DSST exams also benefit students who are already enrolled in a college or university. With college tuition costs on the rise, most students face financial challenges. The fee for each DSST exam starts at $80 (plus administration fees charged by some testing facilities)—significantly less than the $750 average cost of a 3-hour college class. Maximize tuition assistance by taking DSST exams for introductory or mandatory course work. Once you earn a passing score on a DSST exam, you are free to move on to higher-level course work in that subject matter, take desired electives, or focus on courses in a chosen major.

Not only do college students and adult learners profit from DSST exams, but military personnel reap the benefits as well. If you are a member of the armed services at home or abroad, you can initiate your post-military career by taking DSST exams in areas with which you have experience. Military personnel can gain credit anywhere in the world, thanks to the fact that almost all of the tests are available through the internet at designated testing locations. DSST testing facilities are located at more than 500 military installations, so service members on active duty can get a jump-start on a post-military career with the DSST program. As an additional incentive, DANTES (Defense Activity for Non-Traditional Education Support) provides funding for DSST test fees for eligible members of the military.

More than 30 subject-matter tests are available in the fields of Business, Humanities, Math, Physical Science, Social Sciences, and Technology.

Available DSST® Exams

Business	Social Sciences
Business Ethics and Society	A History of the Vietnam War
Business Mathematics	Art of the Western World
Computing and Information Technology	Criminal Justice
Human Resource Management	Foundations of Education
Introduction to Business	Fundamentals of Counseling
Management Information Systems	General Anthropology
Money and Banking	History of the Soviet Union
Organizational Behavior	Introduction to Geography
Personal Finance	Introduction to Law Enforcement
Principles of Finance	Lifespan Developmental Psychology
Principles of Supervision	Substance Abuse
	The Civil War and Reconstruction

Humanities	Physical Sciences
Ethics in America	Astronomy
Introduction to World Religions	Environment Science
Principles of Advanced English Composition	Health and Human Development
Principles of Public Speaking	Introduction to Geology

Math	Technology
Fundamentals of College Algebra	Ethics in Technology
Math for Liberal Arts	Fundamentals of Cybersecurity
Principles of Statistics	Technical Writing

As you can see from the table, the DSST program covers a wide variety of subjects. However, it is important to ask two questions before registering for a DSST exam.

1. Which universities or colleges award credit for passing DSST exams?
2. Which DSST exams are the most relevant to my desired degree and my experience?

Knowing which universities offer DSST credit is important. In all likelihood, a college in your area awards credit for DSST exams, but find out before taking an exam by contacting the university directly. Then review the list of DSST exams to determine which ones are most relevant to the degree you are seeking and to your base of knowledge. Schedule an appointment with your college adviser to determine which exams best fit your degree program and which college courses the DSST exams can replace. Advisers should also be able to tell you the minimum score required on the DSST exam to receive university credit.

DSST® TEST CENTERS

You can find DSST testing locations in community colleges and universities across the country. Check the DSST website (**www.getcollegecredit. com**) for a location near you or contact your local college or university to find out if the school administers DSST exams. Keep in mind that some universities and colleges administer DSST exams only to enrolled students. DSST testing is available to men and women in the armed services at more than 500 military installations around the world.

HOW TO REGISTER FOR A DSST® EXAM

Once you have located a nearby DSST testing facility, you need to contact the testing center to find out the exam administration schedule. Many centers are set up to administer tests via the internet, while others use printed materials. Almost all DSST exams are available as online tests, but the method used depends on the testing center. The cost for each DSST exam starts at $80, and many testing locations charge a fee to cover their costs for administering the tests. Credit cards are the only accepted payment method for taking online DSST exams. Credit card, certified check, and money order are acceptable payment methods for paper-and-pencil tests.

Test takers are allotted two score reports—one mailed to them and another mailed to a designated college or university, if requested. Online tests generate unofficial scores at the end of the test session, while individuals taking paper tests must wait four to six weeks for score reports.

PREPARING FOR A DSST® EXAM

Even though you are knowledgeable in a certain subject matter, you should still prepare for the test to ensure you achieve the highest score possible. The first step in studying for a DSST exam is to find out what will be on the specific test you have chosen. Information regarding test content is located on the DSST fact sheets, which can be downloaded at no cost from **www. getcollegecredit.com**. Each fact sheet outlines the topics covered on a subject-matter test, as well as the approximate percentage assigned to each topic. For example, questions on the Art of the Western World exam are distributed in the following way: Ancient World—15%, Middle Ages—12%, Renaissance—15%, Baroque—10%, Rococo and Neoclassicism—9%, Romanticism and Realism—8%, Impressionism and Post-Impressionism—8%, Early Twentieth Century—12%, Postwar to Postmodern—6%, and Contemporary—5%.

In addition to the breakdown of topics on a DSST exam, the fact sheet also lists recommended reference materials. If you do not own the recommended books, then check college bookstores. Avoid paying high prices for new textbooks by looking online for used textbooks. Don't panic if you are unable to locate a specific textbook listed on the fact sheet; the textbooks are merely recommendations. Instead, search for comparable books used in university courses on the specific subject. Current editions are ideal, and it is a good idea to use at least two references when studying for a DSST exam. Of course, the subject matter provided in this book will be a sufficient review for most test takers. However, if you need additional information, it is a good idea to have some of the reference materials at your disposal when preparing for a DSST exam.

Fact sheets include other useful information in addition to a list of reference materials and topics. Each fact sheet includes subject-specific sample questions like those you will encounter on the DSST exam. The sample questions provide an idea of the types of questions you can expect on the exam. Test questions are multiple-choice with one correct answer and three incorrect choices.

The fact sheet also includes information about the number of credit hours ACE has recommended be awarded by colleges for a passing DSST exam score. However, you should keep in mind that not all universities and colleges adhere to the ACE recommendation for DSST credit hours. Some institutions require DSST exam scores higher than the minimum score recommended by ACE. Once you have acquired appropriate reference materials and you have the outline provided on the fact sheet, you are ready to start studying, which is where this book can help.

TEST DAY

After reviewing the material and taking practice tests, you are finally ready to take your DSST exam. Follow these tips for a successful test day experience.

1. **Arrive on time.** Not only is it courteous to arrive on time to the DSST testing facility, but it also allows plenty of time for you to take care of check-in procedures and settle into your surroundings.

2. **Bring identification.** DSST test facilities require that candidates bring a valid government-issued identification card with a current photo and signature. Acceptable forms of identification include a current driver's license, passport, military identification card, or state-issued identification card. Individuals who fail to bring proper identification to the DSST testing facility will not be allowed to take an exam.

3. **Bring the right supplies.** If your exam requires the use of a calculator, you may bring a calculator that meets the specifications. For paper-based exams, you may also bring No. 2 pencils with an eraser and black ballpoint pens. Regardless of the exam methodology, you are NOT allowed to bring reference or study materials, scratch paper, or electronics such as cell phones, personal handheld devices, cameras, alarm wrist watches, or tape recorders to the testing center.

4. **Take the test.** During the exam, take the time to read each question and the provided answers carefully. Eliminate the choices you know are incorrect to narrow the number of potential answers. If a question completely stumps you, take an educated guess and move on—remember that DSSTs are timed; you will have 2 hours to take the exam.

With the proper preparation, DSST exams will save you both time and money. So join the thousands of people who have already reaped the benefits of DSST exams and move closer than ever to your college degree.

ART OF THE WESTERN WORLD EXAM FACTS

The DSST® Art of the Western World exam consists of 100 multiple-choice questions that assess students for knowledge equivalent to that acquired in an Art of the Western World college course. The exam includes the following topics: Ancient World, Middle Ages, Renaissance, Baroque, Rococo and Neoclassicism, Romanticism and Realism, Impressionism and Post-Impressionism, Early Twentieth Century, Postwar to Postmodern, and Contemporary.

Area or Course Equivalent: Art of the Western World
Level: Lower-level baccalaureate
Amount of Credit: 3 Semester Hours
Minimum Score: 400
Source: https://www.getcollegecredit.com/wp-content/assets/factsheets/
ArtOfTheWesternWorld.pdf

I. **Ancient World – 15%**

   a. Ancient Near East

   b. Egypt

   c. Greece

   d. Rome

II. **Middle Ages – 12%**

   a. Early Christian, Byzantine, and Romanesque

   b. Gothic

III. **Renaissance – 15%**

   a. 15th-Century Italy

   b. 15th-Century Northern Europe

   c. 16th-Century Italy

   d. 16th-Century Northern Europe

IV. **Baroque– 10%**

   a. Italy, France, and Spain

   b. Holland and Flanders

V. **Rococo and Neoclassicism – 9%**

VI. **Romanticism and Realism – 8%**

VII. **Impressionism and Post-Impressionism – 8%**

VIII. **Early Twentieth Century – 12%**

   a. Emergency of Modernism

   b. Art between the World Wars

IX. **Postwar to Postmodern – 6%**

X. **Contemporary – 5%**

Chapter 2

Art of the Western World Diagnostic Test

DIAGNOSTIC TEST ANSWER SHEET

1. Ⓐ Ⓑ Ⓒ Ⓓ

2. Ⓐ Ⓑ Ⓒ Ⓓ

3. Ⓐ Ⓑ Ⓒ Ⓓ

4. Ⓐ Ⓑ Ⓒ Ⓓ

5. Ⓐ Ⓑ Ⓒ Ⓓ

6. Ⓐ Ⓑ Ⓒ Ⓓ

7. Ⓐ Ⓑ Ⓒ Ⓓ

8. Ⓐ Ⓑ Ⓒ Ⓓ

9. Ⓐ Ⓑ Ⓒ Ⓓ

10. Ⓐ Ⓑ Ⓒ Ⓓ

11. Ⓐ Ⓑ Ⓒ Ⓓ

12. Ⓐ Ⓑ Ⓒ Ⓓ

13. Ⓐ Ⓑ Ⓒ Ⓓ

14. Ⓐ Ⓑ Ⓒ Ⓓ

15. Ⓐ Ⓑ Ⓒ Ⓓ

16. Ⓐ Ⓑ Ⓒ Ⓓ

17. Ⓐ Ⓑ Ⓒ Ⓓ

18. Ⓐ Ⓑ Ⓒ Ⓓ

19. Ⓐ Ⓑ Ⓒ Ⓓ

20. Ⓐ Ⓑ Ⓒ Ⓓ

ART OF THE WESTERN WORLD DIAGNOSTIC TEST

24 minutes—20 questions

Directions: Carefully read each of the following 20 questions. Choose the best answer to each question and fill in the corresponding circle on the answer sheet. The Answer Key and Explanations can be found following this Diagnostic Test.

---

1. A philosophy that celebrates human beings and their freedom of thought is known as

   A. capitalism.
   B. verism.
   C. humanism.
   D. realism.

2. The integration of various previous styles in early Christian art is known as

   A. the composite view.
   B. verism.
   C. symbolism.
   D. syncretism.

3. The Baroque period echoed which of the following movements?

   A. Protestantism
   B. Humanism
   C. Absolutism
   D. Realism

4. Which of the following artists best represents art with a social agenda?

   A. Robert Mapplethorpe
   B. Jasper Johns
   C. Andy Warhol
   D. Robert Rauschenberg

5. Which of the following artistic movements softened the seriousness of the Baroque style?

A. Enlightenment
B. Humanism
C. Rococo
D. Neoclassicism

6. The Sumerians invented *cuneiform*, which were

A. stone tablets with inscriptions.
B. the first written symbols.
C. massive stepped towers.
D. votive statuaries.

7. Most of the early Renaissance period centered in which country?

A. France
B. Belgium
C. Italy
D. Germany

8. The Romantic movement is most noted for its celebration of

A. nature.
B. human rights.
C. empiricism
D. social ideals.

9. Which of the following artists is best known for the use of small strokes of color to create form?

A. Edgard Degas
B. Henri de Toulouse-Lautrec
C. Claude Monet
D. Georges Seurat

10. Which of the following architectural devices is best represented in the structure of the cathedral of Notre Dame in France?

A. Vault
B. Flying buttress
C. Crossing square
D. Arch

11. The term *en plein air* refers to what painting style?

   A. Dark spaces, with light to indicate emotion
   B. Painting to show how the artist perceives the subject
   C. Painting on fresh, wet plaster
   D. Painting to capture the atmosphere and lighting of a scene

12. Discoveries from the ancient worlds of Greece and Rome reinforced the artistic movement toward

   A. the Enlightenment.
   B. Neoclassicism.
   C. the Rococo.
   D. painting.

13. What artist is considered foremost in the Cubism painting style?

   A. Paul Cézanne
   B. Georges Braque
   C. Pablo Picasso
   D. Edvard Munch

14. Paintings about scenes that depict everyday people in a natural setting are called

   A. portraits.
   B. genre painting.
   C. still life.
   D. landscapes.

15. Which of the following paintings depicts a straightforward, anti-spiritual attitude towards death?

   A. *The Third of May*
   B. *Burial at Ornans*
   C. *The Massacre at Chios*
   D. *The Death of Sardanapalus*

16. Which of the following is considered a geometric design?

   A. Meander pattern
   B. Doric style
   C. Cycladic style
   D. Contrapposto

17. Which of the following popes commissioned Michelangelo to paint the ceiling of the Sistine Chapel?

   A. Julius II
   B. Leo X
   C. Julius III
   D. Sixtus IV

18. Which of the following has become a leading medium, particularly in contemporary life?

   A. Painting
   B. Architecture
   C. Video
   D. Sculpture

19. The Romans built arches and domes made of

   A. marble.
   B. concrete.
   C. limestone.
   D. wood.

20. What movement emphasized art that is violent, energetic, and bold?

   A. Realism
   B. Futurism
   C. Abstract Cubism
   D. Neoabstractivism

ANSWER KEY AND EXPLANATIONS

1. C	5. C	9. C	13. C	17. A
2. D	6. B	10. B	14. B	18. C
3. C	7. C	11. D	15. B	19. B
4. A	8. A	12. B	16. A	20. B

1. **The correct answer is C.** Humanism is the philosophy that celebrates human beings and their freedom of thought. Capitalism (choice A) is a type of economic system that is based on exchanges for profit. Verism (choice B) and realism (choice D) both signify expressing the truth of existence and creating art that reflects nature.

2. **The correct answer is D.** Syncretism is an integration of previous styles with a new purpose. The composite view (choice A) describes art that is shown in profile. Verism (choice B) is a style of art that focuses on a realistic portrayal of a subject. Symbolism (choice C) is the use of distinct images to express ideas, emotions, and beliefs.

3. **The correct answer is C.** The Counter-Reformation was the impetus of the Baroque period, which emphasized absolutism. Protestantism (choice A) was the result of grievances against the Roman Catholic Church. Humanism (choice B) is a philosophy that celebrates human beings and their freedom of thought. Realism (choice D) promoted the creation of art that reflected nature.

4. **The correct answer is A.** Photographer Robert Mapplethorpe created many black-and-white images that honored people who had been criticized by society. Jasper Johns (choice B), Andy Warhol (choice C), and Robert Rauschenberg (choice D) were all pop artists who focused attention on the mundane aspects of the everyday world without communicating a specific message.

5. The correct answer is C. The Rococo style tended to soften the weightiness of the Baroque period and emphasized a more light-hearted and delicate approach to creativity. The Enlightenment (choice A) was an intellectual movement that placed reason above traditional beliefs. Humanism (choice B) is a philosophy that celebrates human beings and their freedom of thought. Neoclassicism (choice D) is more closely aligned with the Enlightenment's focus on clarity and intellectualism.

6. The correct answer is B. Cuneiform is a type of written language, the first recorded in history. Although the symbols were used on stone tablets (choice A), the symbols could be used with any medium. The Sumerians were also noted for their massive stepped towers (choice C), a form of temple architecture, as well as their votive statuaries (choice D).

7. The correct answer is C. Florence, Italy, was one of the earliest centers of Renaissance art. Rome and Venice were other artistic centers. France (choice A) and Flanders (choice B) were significant locations, but less prominent in the early period. Germany (choice D) became more prominent in the later periods of the Renaissance.

8. The correct answer is A. Romantic art embraced an almost spiritual attachment to the natural world. An emphasis on human rights (choice B), empiricism (choice C), and social ideals (choice D) are all emblematic of Realism.

9. The correct answer is C. Claude Monet was the most passionate follower of the Impressionism movement, which uses dabs of color to create a scene. Edgar Degas (choice A) tended to use linear curves and solid structures, which set him apart from other Impressionists. Henri de Toulouse-Lautrec (choice B) and George Seurat (choice D) were Post-Impressionists.

10. **The correct answer is B.** Gothic designers invented the flying buttress to support ceilings with semi-arches and vertical piers, and it is this architectural device that is best represented in the cathedral of Notre Dame. A vault (choice A) is any roof in the form of an arch. The crossing square (choice C) is evocative of the Romanesque style, which predated the Gothic style. The arch (choice D) was developed during the classical Roman period.

11. **The correct answer is D.** *En plain air* is defined as painting to capture the atmosphere and lighting of a scene. Painting dark spaces with lighting to indicate emotion (choice A) is called Tenebrism. Painting to show the artist's perception of the subject (choice B) is called Mannerism. Painting on fresh, wet plaster (choice C) is known as Fresco painting.

12. **The correct answer is B.** Neoclassicism emphasized an adherence to classical techniques that were reinvigorated after numerous discoveries from the ancient world. The Enlightenment (choice A) was an intellectual movement that placed reason above traditional beliefs. The Rococo (choice C) emphasized delicate decoration and a sense of frivolity. Paintings (choice D) are a medium of art that has been practiced throughout human existence.

13. **The correct answer is C.** Pablo Picasso is considered the foremost artist in the Cubism genre. Georges Braque (choice B) was Picasso's contemporary, but his work was in Analytic Cubism. Paul Cézanne (choice A) was an Impressionist painter, a movement that led eventually to Fauvism, Cubism, and Expressionism. Edvard Munch was an Expressionist painter, reflecting on the inner emotions of the artist.

14. **The correct answer is B.** Genre painting focuses on realistic scenes and ordinary people. Portraits (choice A) are images of people, usually important people, in an elegant setting. Still life paintings (choice C) depict inanimate objects. Landscapes (choice D) are pictures of scenery that can be realistic or impressionistic.

15. The correct answer is B. Courbet's *Burial at Ornans* is a down-to-earth and frank portrayal of death as simply the end of existence. *The Third of May* (choice A) by Goya is a highly dramatic depiction of a cruel execution. *The Massacre at Chios* (choice C) and *The Death of Sardanapalus* (choice D) by Delacroix both depict dramatic events meant to portray the suffering of their subjects.

16. The correct answer is A. The meander pattern, or Greek key pattern, is a geometric design. The Doric style (choice B) is an architectural column style. Cycladic style (choice C) is a simple, abstract style developed by the earliest Greek culture. Contrapposto (choice D) is a sculptural style that emphasizes human movement.

17. The correct answer is A. Julius II is said to have launched the High Renaissance and was the pope who commissioned Michelangelo to paint the Sistine Chapel. Leo X (choice B) and Julius III (choice C) followed Julius II. Sixtus IV (choice D) preceded him.

18. The correct answer is C. Video became a leading medium after the dawn of television and particularly after the introduction of wireless broadcasting and cable. Painting (choice A) has resurged as a medium, but it is not particular to contemporary art. Architecture (choice B) and sculpture (choice D) are also not specific to contemporary life.

19. The correct answer is B. The arches and vaults of the Colosseum could not have been built without concrete. Marble (choice A) was used in Greek and Roman buildings, but it was limited in terms of its architectural capability. Limestone (choice C) by itself is also a stone, however it dissolves over time when exposed. Although wood (choice D) is a building material, buildings made of wood would not have lasted to this day.

20. The correct answer is B. Futurism was started by poet Filippo Marinetti, whose manifesto called for art that was violent, energetic, bold, and free from the boundaries of harmony and good taste. Realism (choice A) called for realistic portrayals, including imperfections. Abstract Cubism (choice C) emphasized lines without conventional form. Neoabstractivism (choice D) is not a real artistic movement.

DIAGNOSTIC TEST ASSESSMENT GRID

Now that you've completed the diagnostic test and read through the answer explanations, you can use your results to focus your studying. Find the question numbers from the diagnostic test that you answered incorrectly and highlight or circle them below. Then, focus extra attention on the sections within Chapter 3 dealing with those topics.

Art of the Western World		
Content Area	**Topic**	**Question #**
Ancient World	• Ancient Near East • Egypt • Greece • Rome	6, 16, 19
Middle Ages	• Early Christian, Byzantine, and Romanesque • Gothic	2, 10
Renaissance	• 15th-Century Italy • 15th-Century Northern Europe • 16th-Century Italy • 16th-Century Northern Europe	1, 7, 17
Baroque	• Italy, France, and Spain • Holland and Flanders	3, 14
Rococo & Neoclassicism	—	5, 12
Romanticism & Realism	—	8, 15
Impressionism & Post-Impressionism	—	9, 11
Early Twentieth Century	• Emergency of Modernism • Art between the World Wars	13, 20
Postwar to Postmodern	—	4
Contemporary	—	18

Chapter 3

Art of the Western World Subject Review

Overview
- Ancient World
- Middle Ages
- Renaissance
- Baroque
- Rococo and Neoclassicism
- Romanticism and Realism
- Impressionism and Post-Impressionism
- Early Twentieth Century
- Postwar to Postmodern
- Contemporary
- Conclusion
- Summing It Up

DSST® Art of the Western World covers the history of art through each of the time periods listed in the Overview. You may or may not be familiar with some of the topics covered, but don't worry. This guide is designed to provide all the material you will see on the DSST exam and provide you with plenty of examples to help your understanding.

ANCIENT WORLD

Ancient Near East

The fertile valley between the Tigris and Euphrates rivers, which the Greeks called **Mesopotamia**, is called the "cradle of civilization." It was here that humans came together to form complex societies based on their farming and irrigation techniques. These **city-states** became urban centers of political, economic, social, religious, and artistic development, evidenced by the many works of art and architecture left behind.

Sumerians

The Sumerians are considered the creators of Mesopotamian civilization. By 3000 B.C.E., they had developed **cuneiform**, the first written symbols, and built temples to honor their gods. These temples were built upon massive stepped towers called **ziggurats**, which represented the link between humans and their gods above. The **White Temple of Uruk** (in present-day Iraq) is a well-preserved example, and it is believed to have been dedicated to the sky god Anu, the greatest of the Sumerian gods.

Ziggurat of Uruk. Source: Library of Congress.

Another aspect of the Sumerians' devotion to their gods was the creation of votive statuary, such as the one shown in the following image. The most distinctive features in the statuaries are the faces with large round eyes, highlighted by inlaid lapis lazuli and shells set in **bitumen**, a viscous material used as an adhesive. The poses and costumes of these figures are seen in later Mesopotamian art.

Standing male worshiper. Source: The Metropolitan Museum of Art; Fletcher Fund, 1940.

Several centuries before the Egyptians built stone pyramids, the Sumerians used mud bricks to build their temples. They also used these mud bricks to build luxurious tombs that encased treasures such as helmets, daggers, beakers, bowls, jewelry, and musical instruments made of gold and lapis lazuli. Probably the most important objects found in one of the tombs is the **Royal Standard of Ur**, a small wooden box inlaid with shells, lapis lazuli, and red limestone depicting the activities of the king and his armies on one side, the reverse showing banquet scenes.

The discovery of special **steles** (upright marker stones carved in relief) and stamp and cylinder seals give evidence to the importance the Sumerians gave to protecting and authenticating ownership. These artifacts exemplify the Sumerians' complex artistic abilities, as well as their advanced trading and commercial practices.

Record of a Sumerian commercial transaction. Source:
The Metropolitan Museum of Art; Funds from various donors, 1958.

Sumerian seal. Source: The Metropolitan Museum of Art;
Bequest of W. Gedney Beatty, 1941.

Akkadians

As the number of city-states grew and expanded, battles occurred over the control of land and water, and threats of invasion were common. The Akkadians, Semitic people who lived to the north of the Sumerians, eventually invaded and conquered most of Mesopotamia. Under the rulership of King Sargon, the Akkadian people established a dynastic empire that adopted much of the Sumerian culture. Visual arts such as sculpture were used to reflect the power of the monarchy. The remains of one such sculpture, a huge hollow-casted copper head of an Akkadian king, was found at Nineveh, an ancient Assyrian city of Upper Mesopotamia, located on the outskirts of Mosul in modern-day Iraq. This sculpture is significant for its reflection of the ruler's godlike dignity, as well as the sculptor's advanced skills of molding, casting, welding, and artistry. The power of the kings of Akkad is evident in the victory stele erected during the rule of Naram-Sin. The stele commemorates the king's victory over an enemy, with the king at the top as the largest figure in relief, powerful and majestic, with his orderly ranks of soldiers below.

Babylonians

Around 2000 B.C.E., invading peoples from Iran conquered Mesopotamia, and the ensuing centuries were a time of turmoil and warfare. The city of Babylon eventually emerged as the center of a centralized government with Hammurabi as its most powerful king. After gaining control of Sumer and Akkad, he left a dynasty strong enough to last for 300 years. Hammurabi is best known for establishing a set of fair and pragmatic rules for his people called **The Code of Hammurabi**, which survives as a tall, black basalt stele. The stele, which records Hammurabi's laws, shows the king in relief at the top of the structure; his hand is lifted in greeting before the sun god, Shamash, who gives him the power to rule and preserve the law.

Other Groups

The Hittites, Assyrians, Neo-Babylonians, and Achaemenids followed the Babylonians, but each adopted and advanced the art and culture of the Sumerians.

Egypt

The rich, lush soil along the Nile river yielded abundant crops and helped develop the civilization of ancient Egypt, a complex and sophisticated society that lasted for 2,000 years. Many of Egypt's great mysteries have been revealed through a pictorial writing system called **hieroglyphics**, which are displayed in the writings, paintings, reliefs, and colossal sculptures and tombs that remain to this day.

The Egyptians were devoted to their king, the **pharaoh**, who was worshiped as divine, along with other gods, subgods, and natural spirits. A deep belief in the afterlife also dominated Egyptian life, and many objects and elaborate paintings were buried with the dead to help them cross over to eternity. Egyptian artists used rich, deep colors and a technique known as a **composite view** to present a profile or side view of people or animals.

Early Dynastic Period

Many aspects of Egyptian civilization developed during the Early Dynastic Period. The surviving art mostly comes from tombs and monuments, and are reflections of the belief of life after death. Reverence to the divine power of the king was stressed through the use of symbols and **hieratic scale**, a manner of using relative size to reflect importance.

Some of the earliest preserved art pieces were created during this period. One such example is the *Palette of King Narmer*, a stone tablet that was likely used to grind paint for an ornamental ceremony. The tablet includes a hieroglyphic inscription identifying the ruler flanked by carved low reliefs of the king and his enemies in profile. The king is relatively large in size, while his enemies are smaller and shown as running away or in supplication.

This period is also important for the oldest elaborate tombs dedicated to the afterlife. One of the earliest known **stepped pyramids** (structures built as receding flat platforms) was designed by the first recorded artist-architect, **Imhotep**, whose name is inscribed together with that of King Djoser on the base of a statue near his tomb.

Step pyramid. Source: Library of Congress.

Old Kingdom

The period of the Old Kingdom is known for its political stability and economic wealth. It is best characterized by the **Pyramids of Giza** (also known as the **Giza Necropolis**), as well as the statuary dedicated to the immortal kings. The Giza Necropolis includes three monumental, flat-sided pyramids with elaborate burial complexes that are considered the greatest architectural achievement of the time. This is also the site of the **Great Sphinx**, a mythical creature with a lion's body and a human head and the largest monolithic statue in the world.

Pyramids and Sphinx at Giza. Source: Library of Congress.

During the period of the Old Kingdom, sculptors created the first life-sized statues and reliefs in stone, copper, and wood that were painted using natural minerals. Statues discovered from this period show that the figures were more lifelike than those from the Early Dynastic Period. Sculptures of Egyptian kings were usually carved in stone to emphasize their permanence, with perfect, idealized bodies rigidly posed to show their dignity.

One of the most well-known of these sculptures is *King Khafre*, who sits on a magnificent throne, looking off into the distance.

Middle Kingdom

During this period, rock-cut tombs were hollowed out of the face of cliffs for wealthy and high-ranking officials. Sculpted portraiture also seemed to be more reflective of human emotions. For example, while the *Head of Senwosret III* reflects the king's majestic authority, the face has an introspective expression, reflecting a troubled yet resolute demeanor. Funerary **stelai** (stone slabs inscribed, carved, or painted with imagery) were commissioned by prosperous citizens to honor the dead. Stelae were also used to publish laws, record historical events, and mark property.

Funeral stela of the bowman Semin with hieroglyphs and composite view.
Source: Metropolitan Museum of Art; Rogers Fund, 1920.

New Kingdom

During this period, many elaborate temples were built to worship the gods or as mortuaries for Egyptian monarchs. This period is considered the golden age of Ancient Egyptian art because prosperity allowed for extensive building along the Nile. Great temple complexes were built with chapels, pylons, obelisks, and great halls decorated with elaborate friezes. **Hatshepsut's (Deir el-Bahri) Temple** is a well-preserved mortuary built for the first female ruler whose name has been recorded. Another well-known temple is the **Amen-Re at Karnak**.

During this New Kingdom era, a ruler named Akhenaton introduced a new religion and new art forms. Royal imagery underwent a drastic change, moving away from an idealistic style to a more flawed or caricaturist portrayal. This break with tradition appeared in paintings as well as sculpture. Two busts that reflect this departure from tradition are the busts of Nefertiti and Tiye. The bust of **Nefertiti**, the wife of Akhenaton, has an exaggerated heavy crown with a long, almost snake-like neck. The idealistic beauty of the face is almost too perfect to be human. In contrast, the miniature head of **Tiye**, Akhenaton's mother, reflects her age, personality, and humanness—another departure from the traditional idealistic style.

Greece

Ancient Greek art is notable for its naturalistic yet idealized representations of the human body, as well as its development of architectural forms that are still seen today. Greek culture, which derived from a belief in the supremacy of human beings, is the basis of Western civilization and the concept of democracy.

Like the Egyptians, the ancient Greeks worshipped gods and goddesses and fervently believed in an afterlife. But unlike the Mesopotamian and Egyptian deities, who were portrayed as magical creatures with animalistic features, the Greek gods had human form. The gods were immortal and all-powerful, but it was believed that humans could become gods if they exemplified the Greek heroic ideal.

Prehistoric Greece

The earliest Greek culture, **Cycladic**, produced simple, abstract marble figurines, such as the one shown next. On the island of Crete, the great **Minoan** civilization followed. Its elaborate, mazelike palaces were adorned with colorful **frescoes**, a technique of painting on fresh, wet plaster. Its pottery, which was thrown from the potter's wheel, was also especially sophisticated. The **Myceneans**, who later conquered Crete, were greatly influenced by Minoan art and culture. They are best known for their skill working with gold and other metals, evidenced by the funerary masks, jewelry, vases, and other objects buried with their dead.

Cycladic seated harp player. Source: Metropolitan Museum of Art; Rogers Fund, 1947.

Geometric Period

The Mycenaean world ended around 1200 B.C.E., followed by a period of poverty and social disintegration known as the Dark Age of Greece. In the eighth century B.C.E, prosperity returned and the Greeks began to trade with civilizations to the east and west. Influenced by Egyptian and Mesopotamian styles, the Greeks created human figurines and painted geometric motifs on pottery. The most famous of these geometric designs is the **meander pattern**, also known as the **Greek key** pattern.

Greek geometric vase. Source: Metropolitan Museum of Art; Rogers Fund, 1912.

Archaic Period

During the Archaic Period, the Greeks created many stone sculptures representing life-size humans and adhering to realistic proportions. Smiles were later added to both male and female statues to make them appear more lifelike. Female figures were usually draped, while male figures were usually nude in celebration of the Olympic athletes.

In architecture, the first **Doric** and **Ionic** styles, or **orders**, appeared in limestone and marble, setting the standards for beauty, harmony, and strength. Doric columns are simple in design, characterized by wide, heavy columns, plain round **capitals** (tops), and no base. Ionic columns are slender and more decorative, with a large base and two elaborate scrolls on either side of the capitals.

During this period, Athenian ceramists also developed **black-figure painting**, which is a technique used during the firing of the clay to decorate vases with silhouetted figures of people and events. (The **red-figure** reversal technique, with its reddish figures against a black background, was developed later.)

Classical Period

The Classical Period in Greek art is reflected by its emphasis on balance and enduring perfection. They applied a standard of proportions for statuary, and mathematical formulas helped achieve harmonious design in architecture. Sculpture began to depict figures as moving or shifting their weight, called **contrapposto**, as evidenced in the statue of *Kritios Boy*, who has one leg forward. Fifty years later, sculptors began to add the appearance of natural movement and expression to the statues they created. An example is the bronze statuette of a youth dancing, shown next.

Bronze statuette of a youth dancing. Source: Metropolitan Museum of Art; Bequest of Walter C. Baker, 1971.

The **Acropolis** was an Athenian citadel rebuilt after Persian armies had sacked it. The most dominant structure, which is still standing, is the **Parthenon** temple. This building is a testament to the Athenian quest for perfect proportions.

The Parthenon. Source: Library of Congress.

Later, architects developed additional building types, shifting the emphasis away from temples to mausoleums and governmental meeting houses. **Corinthian** columns began to replace the Ionic style. These columns are the most elaborately designed order, with their inverted bell shape covered with rows of acanthus leaves and scrolls carved in stone.

Hellenistic Period

Hellenistic architects and sculptors broke away from the symmetry and restraint of the Classical Period, becoming more daring and exploratory. Artists seemed to relish breaking the rules of classical design, depicting riotous confusion and strong emotion rather than clarity and balance. This movement is called **theatricality**, and a good example is the **Temple of Apollo at Didyma**. Its outside appearance looks similar to other classical buildings, but the interior surprises visitors with dramatic vistas and experiences. Hellenistic sculptors emphasized the portrayal of emotion and movement and highlighted the individuality and drama of the subjects they captured. The *Venus de Milo* is a prime example, with her sensuous pose and intense expression.

Rome

The Roman Empire eventually conquered Greece and expanded across the entire region of the Mediterranean. The Romans considered themselves the divinely appointed rulers of the world, and although their art absorbed influences from the Greeks and other cultures, it was uniquely Roman in character. Roman contributions to art, literature, engineering, and politics continue to affect our lives today.

Etruscans

Before the Roman Empire dominated the Italian peninsula, the Etruscans were first to emerge as the dominant culture. Highly skilled mariners, they enriched themselves through trade with the Greeks and other people from the eastern Mediterranean. The confidence they derived from their wealth helped them develop their own rich artistic traditions, which left a permanent impression on the art and architecture of early Rome.

Etruscans are best known for their unique temple designs; the first widespread use of the stone arch; dynamic terracotta statuary; multi-chambered, frescoed tombs; and finely crafted bronze objects and sculpture. An excellent example of the technical sophistication and dynamic ferocity in Etruscan bronze sculpture is the famous *She-Wolf*, which depicts the animal nursing the infants Romulus and Remus (the founders of Rome).

Roman Republic

The Roman Republic was established in the Italian peninsula after the Latin-speaking inhabitants of Rome expelled the Etruscan king in 509 B.C.E. Roman art and architecture derived from its Etruscan heritage but also had a heavy Greek influence.

Roman portraiture emphasized **verism**, an exact likeness of the subject, as is evidenced by the distinct facial features carved into the free-standing stone busts that were created. The subjects were mostly aristocratic men with a distinguished lineage. Roman society was very class oriented and centered upon patron–client relationships whereby wealthier, more powerful patrons cared for lower-class **clients** (dependent citizens).

Marble bust of a man in the realistic style.
Source: Metropolitan Museum of Art; Rogers Fund, 1912.

Elite Roman houses were decorated with elaborate wall paintings that utilized fresco techniques and **mosaics**, images or patterns produced by arranging small colored pieces of stone, tile, or glass. Two painted mural styles have been discovered from this period: the simplest style involves the painting or stucco molding of the wall to imitate masonry blocks; the second style includes architectural features and illusionistic scenes featuring mortals interacting with gods.

Early Empire

The republic ended when Augustus, the first Roman emperor, defeated the forces of Marc Antony and Cleopatra at the Battle of Actium in 31 B.C.E. A new form of **idealism**, distinctly Roman and grounded in reality, was emphasized in the art and architecture during this time. Portrait sculpture became less realistic and more idealized. This is best exemplified in the sculpture known as *Augustus of Prima Porta*, which portrays the aging emperor as young, vibrant, and powerful—the way he wanted to be remembered. Sculpture, both free-standing and relief, became a tool of propaganda that celebrated the empire's grandeur and confirmed the authority of its rulers.

Roman building flourished during this period. While Augustus lavishly used marble, later buildings were made of **concrete**. Concrete allowed the Romans to build **barrel vaults** (an extension of the simple arch, which creates a ceiling over parallel walls); **groin vaults** (formed by intersecting two barrel vaults at right angles); and **hemispheric domes** (a hollow semispherical structure).

The Flavian emperors who followed Augustus built the **Colosseum**, a huge sport amphitheater for Roman citizens. The arches and vaults of the Colosseum and the **Arch of Titus**, which honored a Flavian victory, could not have been built without concrete.

During this period, murals in the homes of prosperous citizens developed into two additional styles. The third style was more decorative than the previous two, focusing on delicate linear motifs rather than architectural illusions or mystery tales. The fourth style was even more intricate, combining the three previous mural styles and including more realistic, multicolored scenes or portraits.

High and Late Empires

As the empire extended and matured, **forums** (city centers containing markets, temples, and monuments) were created. The **Pantheon**, a temple built to honor Mars and Venus, was built. This structure is best known for its vast **rotunda** (circular room) topped with a massive hemispherical dome.

Mosaics were extensively used throughout these periods, imperial statues and funerary sculpture abounded, and relief sculpture became even more prominent.

Marble sarcophagus. Source: The Metropolitan Museum of Art; Gift of Joseph V. Noble.

In the declining years of the empire, the classical style, which focused on naturalism, individuality, and idealism, was rejected in favor of a simpler, less realistic style. Proportions were abandoned for the sake of symbolism, and the artistic emphasis moved from individual power to social cohesiveness and the power of the office. As the political atmosphere became more and more threatened by outside forces, citizens searched for political stability. The best example of this change of emphasis can be seen in the sculpture, *Portrait of the Four Tetrarchs*, which depicts the four rulers who oversaw different regions of the empire embracing one another.

Constantine the Great eventually rose to power and re-established the notion of stability and the single authority of one ruler. The **Arch of Constantine** was commissioned by the Roman Senate to honor him. This monument is especially noted for its use of **spolia**, which is the use of decoration from previously constructed monuments. The original monuments had been dedicated to good emperors of the past and thus represented the confirmation of Constantine's power as a supreme ruler.

The Arch of Constantine. Source: Library of Congress.

Constantine recognized Christianity as a lawful religion, and the influence of this acceptance began to appear in the many churches built after this legalization. The effect of the Christian influence is also dramatically noted in the *Colossus of Constantine*. It combines elements of classic, naturalistic Roman sculpture with a more abstract style and foreshadows the iconic art of the Middle Ages.

MIDDLE AGES

Early Christian, Byzantine, and Romanesque

In 313 C.E., the Edict of Milan gave equal rights to all religious faiths practiced in the Roman Empire. Although its followers had suffered terrible persecution in the first two centuries, Christianity had become widely accepted and was recognized as the official religion just a few years later. Constantine, the first Christian emperor, began an official building program of Christian churches, and the religion flourished. The earliest Christian artworks reflected **syncretism**, an integration of the classic Roman style and Judeo-Christian symbolism. By 395 C.E., however, Constantine's shift of imperial power to Byzantium in the east created a geographical split that drastically affected the development of Christian art.

Early Christian Art

Much of the earliest Christian art is reflected in the **catacombs**, underground burial chambers used by the faithful who had been initially barred from building places of worship. Artists decorated the walls and ceilings with frescoes, the most sophisticated of which can be seen in a ceiling found in the **Catacomb of Priscilla**. Jesus stands in the middle of a large circle, depicted as *The Good Shepherd*, which emphasizes his humanity and symbolizes his love for mankind. It is believed that **symbolism** and metaphors were widely used in early Christian art so that the figures would be ambiguous and only recognized by Christians. One such symbol was the **chi-rho monogram**, which formed the first two letters of *Christos* using the Greek letters for alpha and omega.

As Christianity spread, wealthier followers placed **sarcophagi** (stone coffins) in the catacombs, sculpted with a mix of Old and New Testament themes. The sculptures adapted pagan motifs and continued to use symbols to signify Christ and his followers.

Sarcophagus lid depicting Christ at Last Judgement.
Source: Metropolitan Museum of Art; Rogers Fund, 1924.

An official building program of churches and **basilicas** (buildings based on Roman civic buildings) emerged, designed to accommodate large congregations. The first, **St. Peter's Basilica**, believed to have been built over the saint's remains, was dedicated by Constantine in 326 C.E. These places of worship were usually decorated with mosaics, such as the burial chapel at **Sta Costanza**, which is supposed to have been dedicated to Constantine's daughter. Much of the mosaic imagery used here is symbolic, but the mosaics lining the **apse** (a semicircular space where the altar was placed) depict Christ giving the keys of heaven to St. Peter and the laws of the church to St. Paul.

The most extensive early Christian mosaics can be found in Ravenna, Italy, where the capital of the western Roman Empire was established in 402 C.E. The **Mausoleum of Galla Placidia** is famous for its rich mosaics depicting Christ as *The Good Shepherd*, now clothed in gold and royal purple and haloed with a circle of light. The departure from classical naturalism to a depiction of the majesty and richness of the spiritual world reflects the shift to a Byzantine influence.

Byzantine Period

In 476 C.E., the western Roman Empire fell to the Visigoths, a Germanic tribe from northern Europe, and entered a period often referred to as the Dark Ages. As the transfer of imperial authority moved to Byzantium (eventually renamed Constantinople), so did many artists and craftsmen, who created a new style of Christian art with strong Greek and Egyptian influences. Byzantine art and architecture focused on religious expression and primarily used mosaics and **icons** (paintings of a religious figure or scene on wooden panels) to convey Orthodox Christian beliefs.

Mosaic icon of the Virgin and Child. Source: Metropolitan Museum of Art; Gift of John C. Weber, in honor of Phillippe de Montebello, 2008.

The **Church of St. Sophia** (also known as the **Hagia Sophia**) in Constantinople is a prime example of Byzantine architecture. Built for the emperor **Justinian** between 532 and 637, it combines the longitudinal shape of a Roman basilica with a domed central plan. Although the building's exterior was simple, the interior was noted for its beautiful mosaics, which were later covered over after the Islamic Turkish occupation. However, the church of **San Vitale** in Ravenna, which was also built during the reign of Justinian, still reflects the stunning beauty of Byzantine mosaic art. The mosaic- and marble-covered walls are bursting with color and inlayed gold that nearly overwhelm the architecture. The mosaics emphasize the majesty of the supernatural, as well as the devotion and supremacy of the state ruler Justinian.

Byzantine icons are also a hallmark of this period, usually created with **encaustic** (heated wax) paint. These works of art were likewise meant to inspire believers, using a symbolic rather than a naturalistic perspective. Halos were painted on Jesus, angels, and the saints to reinforce their sanctity, and figures were always face forward with no sense of three-dimensionality. Special colors were also used to convey meaning, such as red for divinity and blue for humanity. Icons were so prominent and admired during the sixth and seventh centuries that **iconoclasts** began to suspect that the images were being worshipped, even though their primary function was to aid meditation. To this day, the Orthodox Church continues to produce icons to educate and encourage believers.

Ivory carving and manuscript **illumination** (small paintings on vellum by monk-artists to illustrate gospel manuscripts) were also important forms of art during the Byzantine era. The oldest gospel illuminations are the *Garima Gospels*, which are still housed in the Garima Monastery in Ethiopia.

A revival of the culture in the western world was ushered in around the year 775 CE at the royal court of King Charlemagne. This period was influenced by Roman and Byzantine traditions and produced a number of superb illuminated gospel texts. Monasticism became predominant, and immense churches and cathedrals were built. Charlemagne was focused on modeling his kingdom on that of the Roman Empire, and his goal was to combine the ancient imperial ideal with Christianity.

Romanesque Period

After Charlemagne's death, internal and external forces threatened the existence of the Holy Roman Empire. However, Carolingian ideals were carried on in the architectural and art styles that followed. The most important structure built at this time was the **Church of St. Michael** in Hildesheim, Germany, which served as the basis for Romanesque architecture. The bronze doors completed for this cathedral are best known for their relief images from the Book of Genesis on the left door and the life of Jesus on the right door. The ceiling of the church is decorated with fresco. Most important for the Romanesque and Gothic architecture that followed was the **crossing square**, which is the area of overlap between the **nave** (the central part of the church extending longitudinally from the entrance) and the **transept** (structures projecting from the nave that form a cross shape).

The **Romanesque** period derives its name from the Roman-like architectural style that was used to build many European churches between 1050 and 1200 CE. Hundreds of new churches and monasteries were built during this time period to celebrate the primacy of the Christian faith. One of the most famous examples is the **Cathedral of Pisa**, known for its leaning tower. Even though the term *Romanesque* was applied to all art forms during this period, it was influenced by many styles, not just Roman. The style varied in character from region to region, but what remained common was the use of stone masonry in the construction. Tall square, circular, or octagonal towers often marked the church as the most important structure in the community, and the messages of Christianity were echoed through the sculptures that adorned church **portals** (church entryways adorned with a semicircular arch).

Romanesque portal. Source: Metropolitan Museum of Art; Fletcher Fund, 1947.

Another example of early Romanesque style is the **Church of Saint Vincent** in the Catalan castle of Cardona. To strengthen the walls and enrich their presence, masons added bands of stonework to create a series of transverse arches that divided the nave into separate bays. Builders used the rounded arches and barrel vaults of the classic Roman period, but they also introduced changes. Columns were replaced with pillars, thick walls filled empty spaces, and the elevation was divided into three or four levels. The major change that evolved through the advancement of building techniques was the **vaulted ceiling**. Three major types have been identified: (1) tunnel vaults without galleries over the aisles, (2) tunnel vaults with galleries, and (3) a series of raised domes.

In Romanesque architecture, sculpture served only as a final touch. The subordination of ornament to structure is evidenced in the relatively few reliefs or statues. The *Creation and Fall of Adam and Eve* is one exception, shown as an intricate façade by Wiligelmo at the **Modena Cathedral**.

Gothic

A new style of architecture developed in France in the middle of the twelfth century replacing the Romanesque style with soaring pointed arches, thin walls, and huge stained-glass windows that lighted the interiors. The **Benedictine Abbey of Saint-Denis**, just north of Paris, is considered the first Gothic building, but the **Notre Dame Cathedral** with its massive **rose windows** is considered the perfect example of Gothic style. The natural light coming through the richly colored glass windows provides an almost heavenly interior light. The following piece is an example of the French stained-glass style used, which is on view at the Metropolitan Museum of Art.

French stained-glass window. Source: Metropolitan Museum of Art;
The Cloisters Collection, 1936.

Gothic designers eliminated the need for thick walls to hold up ceilings by inventing other reinforcement techniques, such as the **flying buttress** that supported ceilings with semi-arches and vertical piers. This innovation in architecture allowed a completely new type of interior to emerge. Between 1250 and 1400 C.E., statues became more independent of their architectural setting throughout Europe, especially in France and Germany. The most representative statues are housed in the **Naumburg** and **Bamberg Cathedrals** of Germany, which feature emotionally expressive figures dramatically posed.

The French Gothic style also influenced English architecture. **Westminster Abbey** and the **Salisbury Cathedral** are two such examples. However, these structures differ from the French style with their wider and shorter facades, more horizontal prominence of the nave, and less frequent use of flying buttresses.

RENAISSANCE

The **Renaissance** (literally meaning "rebirth") is considered the artistic and intellectual link between the Middle Ages and contemporary times. The fourteenth century ushered in a renewed focus on **humanism**, a philosophy that honored human nature, just as the classic Romans and Greeks had done before them. Movement away from Byzantine spirituality converted to a focus on the natural world and its beauty.

By the fifteenth century, political and economic developments created a class of higher-status families who acquired their wealth through commerce rather than by their position in a royal hierarchy. Centers of trade were flourishing in Northern Europe and Italy, and **capitalism** (exchange handled by private individuals for profit) became the dominant economic system. The prosperity that unfolded encouraged a renewed interest in a world of art that became a synthesis of classic ideals, religious devotion, and innovative concepts about how society should be governed.

Fifteenth-Century Italy

Florence

In Florence, which had become a center of banking, there were many early humanists who espoused republican ideals and believed that the rule of law should be in the hands of its citizens. Wealthy citizens commissioned buildings and artistic projects for the city and began to compete among themselves to see which patrons would produce the best works. The **Medici** family became the most prominent patrons of the arts, and their influence on Florentine art would last for three centuries.

The earliest Renaissance art was created as a result of competitions, such as who would win the right to decorate the bronze doors of the **Florentine Baptistery**. The two finalists, whose submissions still survive, were **Filippo Brunelleschi** and **Lorenzo Ghiberti**. Although some historians declared the competition a tie, Ghiberti was commissioned to create another set of doors, which he made so artistically perfect that Michelangelo later proclaimed them *"The Gates of Paradise."* For those doors, Ghiberti used Brunelleschi's technique of **linear**, or **one-point**, **perspective** (all lines converging to a single point in the distance), creating a three-dimensional illusion on a two-dimensional surface.

Bronze panels from Ghiberti's *"The Gates of Paradise."* Source: Library of Congress.

Brunelleschi went on to specialize in architecture, measuring buildings in ancient Rome to understand classical proportions. He designed the dome of the **Florence Cathedral**, considered a spectacular feat of engineering. He also completely broke free of Medieval style with the **loggia** (a sheltered room with one or more open sides) that he constructed for the **Ospedale degli Innocenti (Hospital of the Innocents)**. This is considered the first building constructed in early Renaissance style, with its harmonious open spaces defined by arches and supported with Corinthian columns.

Donatello, a sculptor who was a close friend of Brunelleschi, revived the classical principles of working with stone in his statue of *St. George*, which is remarkable for its very realistic depiction of a figure both courageous and concerned about the future. The psychological intensity of Donatello's works made him one of the most renowned sculptors of the early Renaissance. Donatello's *David* is another famous work, the first free-standing male sculpture produced since antiquity. The influence of Greek and Roman style is evident in the detachment of the sculpture from architecture, its depiction of movement (**contrapposto**), and its focus on an accurate and realistic representation of the human body.

Masaccio's fresco paintings are also emblematic of early Renaissance style, with his adoption of the linear perspective giving the impression of three-dimensional reality. His altarpiece, *The Holy Trinity*, is famous for its use of mathematical perspective, as well as its technique of **chiaroscuro** (the use of light and shadow); its realistic portrayal of emotion; and its uncluttered, open arrangement. Two other fresco masterpieces by Masaccio are found in the **Church of Santa Maria del Carmine**, in Florence, Italy. *Tribute Money* is a fresco that depicts three scenes of the life of Jesus in a highly realistic, storytelling style, suggesting a passage of time, and the *Expulsion of Adam and Eve from Eden* displays the artist's superior ability to render human form and depth of emotion.

Another famous Florentine artist was **Botticelli**, who frequently worked for the Medici family and created many secular paintings that resembled sculptural figures. His distinct style, which placed more importance on the human figure than on space, is exemplified in the paintings *Primavera* and *The Birth of Venus*. He would later become important to the **Pre-Raphaelites** of the nineteenth century, who celebrated the beauty and simplicity of his art.

Fifteenth-Century Northern Europe

A cultural Renaissance also occurred north of the Alps, in German-speaking countries, the Lowlands of the Netherlands, France, and England. Although it was influenced by Italian art and the classic style, celebrating human and secular values, this artistic and intellectual movement was distinct and unique. It stressed the idea that individuals were free and that human beings could think for themselves, which ultimately led the way to the Reformation. The invention of the printing press also made the knowledge of classical art, history, and scholarship more readily available.

Flanders and France

As cities in the north prospered, the elite began to support artists and encourage new works of art. Flemish artists that are most notable include Jan van Eyck and Robert Campin. **Jan van Eyck** was remarkable for his mastery of technique in the portrait of *Giovanni Arnolfini and His Wife*. It is one of the first paintings of a secular nature, realistically depicting ordinary objects in the Flemish household that carried significant meaning. To the artist and his world, the single candle represented the unity of husband and wife, the small dog symbolized fidelity, and the oranges on the windowsill and green of the bride's dress connotated fertility.

Robert Campin (also known as the Master of Flémalle) was another artist who adopted the Flemish emphasis on symbolism. His *Mérod Altarpiece*, a three-panel painting (called a **triptych**) in jewel-like colors, represented the Annunciation of Mary in realistic detail, and included ordinary Flemish objects of the time to signify religious concepts.

In France, **Claus Sluter** oversaw the construction of the elaborate *Well of Moses*, an imposing limestone sculpture depicting the Old Testament prophets cloistered together to form a pedestal for a larger work from the New Testament. The first impression of this monument may seem Gothic, but the style is significantly different, in that Suter skillfully differentiated and made unique each of the prophets.

The artistic **illumination** of manuscripts continued during this time. The **Limbourg Brothers** created the most famous work, *Les Trés Riches Heures du Duc de Berry*, for a French duke, depicting figures and events that held special significance to him. Although the manuscript was meant to be a religious prayer book, the themes were highly humanistic—yet another example of the Renaissance blending of religious and secular life.

Folio from *Les Trés Riches Heures dur Duc de Berry* depicting the duke on a journey.
Source: Metropolitan Museum of Art.

Germany

Many painters in the fifteenth century in Germany continued to follow a more ornamental Gothic style rather than the simpler classic style. Their oil paintings represented the world as they perceived it, more realistically and less idealistically. Others were influenced by the southern Renaissance, but they preferred creating wooden panel paintings rather than frescoes. In general, northern artists used wood rather than stone for sculpturing and printmaking.

The *Miraculous Draft of Fishes*, an altarpiece by **Konrad Witz**, is coned the earliest realistic depiction of landscape based on personal observation. He sets the scene of Jesus appearing to the apostles as they fish on the actual Lake of Geneva, painstakingly recording every detail of the natural world that surrounded it.

Arguably, however, the most influential character of the early German Renaissance was **Johannes Gutenberg**, who invented the printing press. His invention allowed more people access to the written word and quickly spread Renaissance ideas and humanistic thinking throughout the world. The *Gutenberg Bible* was the first book printed using moveable type, and it changed the intellectual, spiritual, and artistic world in Europe forever after. The *Nuremberg Chronicle* was published later, and it included almost 2,000 woodcut illustrations. Some wealthy book owners also had their books hand colored after printing.

Sixteenth-Century Italy

During the sixteenth century, Italy was still fervently Roman Catholic, and the pope was not only the leader of the religion but head of state. **Julius II**, who took his name from the Roman statesman, Julius Caesar, was determined to emphasize his power and secure his legacy by once again glorifying Rome. While his predecessor, Sixtus IV, had already enlisted Florentine artists like Botticelli to work at the Vatican, it was Julius II who is said to have launched the **High Renaissance** in Rome in 1503. The Medici family also produced four popes (Leo X, Clement VII, Paul III, and Julius III) who would continue this trend.

The three great artists of this period who were very much in demand were **Leonardi da Vinci, Raphael**, and **Michelangelo**. The humanistic concept of the artist as a divinely inspired being required these artists to be educated in the classics and mathematics, as well as in the crafts they produced. They became famous for their work and travelled extensively, increasing their demand in both the religious and secular worlds.

Leonardo da Vinci

Leonardo da Vinci is widely considered a genius because of his superlative skills in many areas, including engineering, the natural sciences, music, and art. His paintings have become hallmarks of the High Renaissance because the works masterfully synthesized realism with artistic harmony. In his fresco of *The Last Supper*, da Vinci combined classical geometric balance and Renaissance humanism by portraying Jesus as a calm and restrained visual center between the bewildered and animated apostles seated on either side. He also used a balanced **linear structure** (in this case, pyramidal) in his oil painting of the *Virgin of the Rocks*, deftly applying the technique of **chiaroscuro** (a blending of light and shade) to reflect three-dimensional reality. Leonardo also used gradations of color and shade in his realistic portrait of the *Mona Lisa*, but he moved beyond strict realism to a sense of mystery through the subject's subtle expression and the hazy landscape behind her.

Michelangelo

Michelangelo's sculptures of *David*, the *Pietà,* and his *Sistine Chapel* frescoes stand as emblems of the depth and breadth of his artistry. The subject of the *Pietà*, Mary holding her dead son Jesus in her lap, was a common theme in earlier French and German art. Yet Michelangelo's sculpture shows a deep sadness and beauty that has never been surpassed. His choice of **Carrara marble** was especially important to him because he believed that he only needed his sculpturing tools to release the figure that was already in existence within the marble. His *David* is probably his most famous sculpture, embodying the idea of the classic Greek nude, but depicting an emotional and psychological intensity that was completely new.

Pope Julius II believed that Michelangelo's artistic talent would benefit his papacy, so he commissioned him to paint the ceiling of the Sistine Chapel, a **trompe l'oeil** (a visual illusion of a three-dimensional object) depicting theological events. The most familiar scene on the ceiling is the *Creation of Adam* where God grants Adam life. Michelangelo adapted Adam's pose from one he had viewed of an ancient Roman river god, but Adam's heroic body and outstretched arm directly mirror that of God's powerful figure to emphasize that Adam was created in God's image.

Raphael

About the time that Leonardo was working on the *Mona Lisa*, **Raphael Santi** came to Florence and quickly became successful painting portraits of Mary and the baby Jesus. *The Small Cowper Madonna* depicts young Mary with her baby, while the *Madonna of the Meadow* and the *Madonna of the Goldfinch* are two other pieces depicting Mary with the infants Jesus and John the Baptist. Raphael's indebtedness to Leonardo da Vinci is apparent in his adoption of the pyramid structure, tilting of the figure's heads, brilliant colors, and peaceful serenity, as seen in his painting of the *Madonna and Child Enthroned with Saints*.

Raphael's *Madonna and Child Enthroned with Saints*.
Source: Metropolitan Museum of Art; Gift of J. Pierpont Morgan, 1916.

Raphael is also known for his pendant portraits of *Agnelo Doni* and *Maddalena Strozzi*, who are depicted face front before a meticulously rendered landscape. These portraits somewhat echo that of the *Mona Lisa* but differ substantially in that the subjects show little emotional expression and their clothing is colorful and sumptuous. One of Raphael's most important works in terms of representing the High Renaissance era is his *Philosophy (The School of Athens)*, a fresco that exemplifies an ease and familiarity with classical thought and architecture, ordered space, and a melding of religious and human perspectives.

Mannerism

Artists later built on the styles of Raphael and Michelangelo, developing what became known as **mannerism**. However, rather than base their art on the natural world as Raphael and Michelangelo did, mannerist artists seemed to prioritize copying art instead. Artists no longer duplicated what they saw with their own eyes but imitated what they perceived as artistic. This resulted in a distortion of figures, flat, almost two-dimensional spaces, lack of a geometric focal point, and a jarring combination of colors.

Architecture

Architecture once again flourished during the High Renaissance, with the building of the new **St. Peter's Basilica** in Rome. The architect, **Bramante**, designed a central-domed space with a floor plan in the shape of a Greek cross. However, Bramante died before he could execute his plan, and Michelangelo was later commissioned to carry on his work. Michelangelo adopted Bramante's plan but added a ribbed arch dome, undulating façade, and huge pilasters. It took almost a century for the church to be completed by **Gian Lorenzo Bernini**. Michelangelo only lived to see the completion of the drum that was used to support his dome, which was eventually erected some 25 years later by **Giacomo della Porta**.

Andrea Palladio was another leading architect of the period who was influenced by the classical style as it was implemented in ancient Rome. The **Palazzo Chiericati** in Vicenza, the Venetian church of **San Giorgio Maggiore**, and the secular **Villa Rotunda** reflect his faithfulness to the classic style, while also being innovative and daring. Many manor houses in England and the United States later adopted the Palladio style of using a central dome for secular buildings.

Sixteenth-Century Northern Europe

The European world outside Italy, though influenced by the Italian Renaissance, began to change due to the growing power of large centralized states in France, Spain, and England. The Protestant Reformation also profoundly affected the regions of Germany, Austria, Hungary, and the Czech Republic. The spread of this faith disintegrated the unity of Central Europe and led to wars that finally ended in 1555 in a compromise called the **Peace of Augsburg.**

Spain and France

Not all regions converted to the Protestant faith. Spain and France and some regions of central Europe continued to be Roman Catholic. The **Ecole de Fontainebleau,** which refers to two periods of French art, centered on the building of the French royal palaces and was heavily influenced by Italian mannerism. The Spanish empire also extended throughout western Europe at this time, and its art is also reflective of Italian and Flemish influences.

Jean Clouet was an official portrait painter for the French court. His portrait of *Francis I* is known for its dramatic use of space, as if the greatness of the king could not be contained. Although there is great detail and rich color in the painting, there is little attention to realism, with its exaggerated rendering of surfaces and textures.

El Greco is probably the most well-known artist of the Spanish Renaissance and is regarded as the precursor of Expressionism and Cubism because of his highly dramatic and expressive style. He stressed imagination and intuition over the classical criteria of measure and proportion, and he regarded color as having more importance than form. One of his most famous paintings is *The Burial of the Count of Orgaz,* which combines mysticism and realism.

Germany

The conflict between religion and humanism in Northern Europe greatly influenced the development of the visual arts. In the sixteenth century, the art reflected the conflicting beliefs and styles that dominated the period. The invention of the printing press also played a major part in the conflict.

Albrecht Dürer was one of the most prominent artists from Germany, most noted for his drawing, printmaking, and engravings. Although

Dürer was sympathetic to the goals of the Protestant Reformation, his art was very much influenced by Italian styles, classical ideals, and the idea of the artist as a creative genius. His *Self-Portrait* oil painting suggests an almost Christ-like figure, with his penetrating gaze and solemn, self-important expression. It reflects the artist's preference for precise detail and linear perspective, but it does not model the light and shade used by Italian artists. Some believe this is because of his training as a goldsmith and engraver. Ultimately, he would become most well known for his printmaking and his woodcut illustration of *The Four Horseman of the Apocalypse*, based on the Book of Revelation, and the meticulous detail in his engraving of *Adam and Eve*.

Matthias Grünewald is another important figure of the northern Renaissance. Unlike Dürer, he rejected the classical ideals of the Italian Renaissance and focused on traditional religious themes using realism, symbolism, and passionate emotion. In his painting of the *Crucifixion* panel in the *Isenheim Altarpiece*, he used numerous details to depict the anguish of Christ's death. This image of torture is so exaggerated and so far removed from the Renaissance notion of idealistic beauty that it can almost be considered a repudiation. The idea of realistic perspective has also been abandoned, with the figure of Christ dominating the scene and clearly relatively larger than the other figures on the panel.

Albrecht Dürer's *Adam and Eve*. Source: Metropolitan Museum of Art; Fletcher Fund, 1919.

Albrecht Altdorfer painted quite a few religious scenes, but he tended to focus more on the landscape elements of the subject. In many cases, the landscapes dominated the composition almost as if to say that the trials of mankind could be dwarfed by the magnificence of nature.

The Netherlands

After the Reformation, the Netherlands was split into two territories, north and south, with the south remaining Catholic and the north Protestant. Art commissioned during this time period reflected the religious differences of the two partitions. One of the most famous artists of this period was **Hieronymus Bosch**, who was known for using the fantastic imagery that can be seen in his *Garden of Earthly Delights*.

Peter Bruegel the Elder, another important artist from the latter half of the century, was known for combining a love of landscape with slice-of-life scenes. His oil painting, *The Triumph of Death*, is filled with horrific images to emphasize that the nature of death is indiscriminate, with no one spared. In contrast, his *Hunters in the Snow* shows quite a peaceful landscape and celebrates the order and purpose of human life and its integration with nature.

England

English artists were virtually cut off from the European continent, which produced a kind of isolation that was reinforced by nationalistic pride. One of the few foreign painters commissioned to work in England was **Hans Holbein the Younger**, who painted a wedding portrait of *King Henry VIII* in 1540 and *Anne of Cleves* around the same time. The most widely-known, English-born painter of the period was **Nicholas Hilliard**, best known for his miniature portraits. Hilliard's *Ermine Portrait of Queen Elizabeth I* is notable for its sumptuous attention to detail emphasizing the queen's importance, wealth, and power.

BAROQUE

During the seventeenth century, the separation between the Roman Catholic and Protestant churches grew deeper. In seeking to regain the power it had lost, the Roman Catholic Church began a movement known as the **Counter-Reformation**, a passionate defense and declaration of its authority as the universal church. At the **Council of Trent** (a meeting of church leaders held between 1545 and 1563), the Church reaffirmed the dogmas that Protestantism had challenged and called on artists to reinforce the majesty and supremacy of its position.

As a result, the **Baroque** style was born, combining Renaissance classicism with an exuberant theatricality, complexity, and opulence. The goal was to deliver a message of **absolutism** and unlimited grandeur and to inspire followers to remain faithful to the Church.

Italy, France, and Spain

The Baroque era was born in Rome where a series of powerful popes had tremendous influence over politics and art. In France, however, it was the monarchy that sought to convey its majesty and power, heavily influencing the Baroque style. Also, during this time, Spain had become wealthy due to the discovery of the New World and its many resources. The Spanish court generously supported the arts and commissioned painters and sculptors from all over Europe. In general, the art in these three countries adhered to the concepts of classicism, emphasizing order, authority, and tradition.

Italy

The power of the papacy is most evident in the changes that came about during the expansion and renovation of **St. Peter's Basilica** in Vatican City, Rome. Almost every important artist was associated with this effort, which finally culminated in its completion in the seventeenth century. In the church's efforts to emphasize the supremacy of its rule, many other churches were built during this time period as well.

Vatican and St. Peter's, Rome. Source: Library of Congress.

The Baroque style in Rome adopted characteristics of classism but also expanded it to include more ornamentation and drama. The simple, geometric forms of the early Renaissance period were abandoned. **Carlo Maderno** oversaw the first Baroque additions to St. Peter's, enlarging the nave and completing the façade. **Gian Lorenzo Bernini** later designed a massive canopy structure, called a **baldacchino (baldachin)**, over St. Peter's tomb with twisted bronze columns that are nearly 100 feet high.

Painted Baroque ceilings were also highly representative of this era. Ceiling paintings in churches, chapels, and private homes were intended to reflect the power and extravagance of the site. Famous ceiling painters of the time were **Annibale Carraci**, who painted the frescoes in the **Palazzo Farnese** in Rome, and **Giovanni Battista Gaulli**, who painted the ceiling of **Il Gesu**, the mother church of the Jesuits (an order of the Church founded and dedicated to defending the faith).

One of Bernini's rivals in architecture was **Francesco Borromini**, who provided a Baroque alternative style that incorporated elaborate and complex structures resembling sculpture. The interior view of the dome and walls of the church of **Sant'Ivo** are in an oval honeycomb pattern that is highly geometric and subdivided, reflecting the light sources below and avoiding the need for ceiling paintings to focus the eye upward.

Caravaggio (Michelangelo Merisi) was foremost among the painters in Italy during this time period, but he was an extremely controversial figure in his day, prone to gambling and living on the edge. He brought other elements to the Baroque style, emphasizing the earthier, more realistic, and gloomy elements of the human condition. He used light and shade in a dramatic way, incorporating a very dark background, a technique called **tenebrism**, and lighting to accentuate the subject's feelings and humanity. In his oil painting of *The Calling of St. Matthew,* a bright light comes from a mysterious source at the right of the canvas, half-shading Jesus as he points to the young St. Matthew, bathed in the light, as he draws back in fear.

One of Caravaggio's most important followers was **Artemisia Gentileschi**, who closely followed his style and is famous for her rendering of *Judith Beheading Holofernes*, which is grisly in its detail and dramatically lit—emphasizing the heroism and strength of the female biblical figure.

France

The Baroque period in France began to overshadow Rome as the center of the art world. Under the "Sun King" Louis XIV, who believed that his authority was given by God, France developed into a world power. The official court style of art and architecture was derived from the classical world and emphasized the supremacy and absolute rule of the monarchy. It also adopted some of the high drama and energy of the Italian Baroque style.

Louis XIV's preference for the classic style is reflected in the *Palace of Versailles*, which eventually became the center of the royal court. The two most renowned architects of Versailles were **François Mansart** and **Louis Le Vau**. The interior design was overseen by **Charles Le Brun**, and the landscape designer was **Andre Le Notre**.

Because the French believed that mathematics was the basis for beauty, the external facade was designed to be more restrained in expression than the Italian style, with an emphasis on order and regularity. At the same time, however, the interiors were highly dramatic and extravagant. The interior *Hall of Mirrors* combined architectural symmetry with grandiose walls of reflective glass, and rooms throughout the palace were decorated in colorful fabrics, moldings, and marble. The gardens were designed to be spectacular and immense, covering nearly 2,000 acres of land and featuring orderly paths between the flower beds known as **parterres**.

Two of the most important French Baroque painters were **Nicholas Poussin** and **Georges de La Tour**. Both artists exemplified the stylistic polarity of the French Baroque era. Nicholas Poussin combined the French preference for restraint with his strong admiration for classical antiquity. His oil painting of *The Rape of the Sabine Women* reflects his study of ancient sculptures and musculature, while his landscapes, such as the *Landscape* *with St. Mathew and the Angel* and the *Landscape with St. John on Patmos*, are organized as gently illuminated, idealized compositions featuring peaceful classical themes. On the other hand, Georges de La Tour was heavily influenced by Caravaggio, with his extensive use of light for dramatic effect. *The Penitent Magdalene* is one of his most famous works.

The Penitent Magdalen by Georges de La Tour.
Source: Metropolitan Museum of Art; Gift of Mr. and Mrs. Charles Wrightsman.

Spain

Seventeenth-century Spanish painting was heavily influenced by Caravaggio and the Italian Baroque style. It contained a mysticism and religiosity that were encouraged by Spain's strongly Catholic monarchy and aristocracy. The Spanish court not only encouraged native artistic talent, but also supported painters and sculptors from all over Europe.

Diego Velàzquez was the most renowned painter to emerge from the artistic culture of Seville. His subjects were mostly secular, and he preferred the harsh realism that was exemplified in Caravaggio's style, rejecting the more idealistic classic style of the Renaissance. Although his paintings were baroquely colorful, a harsh realism was displayed in the common facial types and naturalistic attitudes reflected in his characters, such as in the *Water Carrier of Seville*. As a court painter for King Philip IV, he was in high demand for his **portraits** (images of faces) of important figures throughout Europe.

Maria Teresa, Infanta of Spain, by Velazquez.
Source: Metropolitan Museum of Art; The Jules Bache Collection, 1949.

Velàzquez also painted many scenes depicting historical and cultural events. *The Surrender at Breda* depicts a gracious and restrained interchange between the opposing forces in celebration of the Spanish victory. One of his most famous paintings is the *Las Meninas (The Maids of Honor)*, where he boldly paints himself into the composition. This group portrait is mysterious in its intent and has stirred up much debate. Although the central figure is clearly the illuminated five-year-old Princess Margarita (the Infanta) surrounded by her attendants, Velàzquez himself is present standing at his easel dressed as a courtier.

Another Spanish painter heavily influenced by Caravaggio and the Italian masters was **Zurbaràn**, who devoted himself to the artistic expression of religion and faith. His painting, *The Birth of the Virgin*, exemplified the strong religious devotion that permeated Spanish art to support the Counter-Reformation. He was also known for his **still life** paintings (a work of art depicting inanimate subjects). All his subjects were treated with a reverence that can be considered uniquely Spanish. His *Still Life with Lemons* detailed the tactile features and color of ordinary natural and manmade objects, but the artist set them against a dramatically dark background that made them seem almost magnificent in their simplicity.

Flanders and Holland

The Baroque of Flanders and Holland was heavily influenced by the religions practiced within these regions. The northern section (present-day Holland) accepted Protestantism, whereas the southern section (Flanders) continued to practice the Catholic faith.

Flanders

The art of **Peter Paul Rubens** best exemplifies Flemish Baroque art. He was heavily influenced by the Italian Baroque style, with his use of the chiaroscuro technique and his vivid representation of movement. However, he integrated a Flemish focus with his choice of colors and intricate details. His paintings of *The Rape of the Daughters of Leucippus*, *The Massacre of the Innocents*, and *The Raising of the Cross* most clearly reflect his focus on "stop-action" dramatic energy, with its theatrical interplay of dark and light colors and passionate feeling. Rubens was also known for his diagonal compositions, representation of full-bodied female nudes, and portraiture.

Ruben's most famous pupil was **Anthony Van Dyck**, who became a specialist in portraiture because of the technical skill he developed collaborating with Ruben. Although he painted religious subjects occasionally, he is most notable for his sympathetic portraiture, which blended a faithful yet idealistic representation of the subject. One of the best examples of this is his portrait of *Charles I at the Hunt*.

Another Flemish artist, **Clara Peeters**, specialized in still life paintings. She reflected the Baroque style with her interplay of light and dark shading, combination of luxurious and everyday objects, and focus on intricate detail. She is best known for her work, *Still Life with Flowers, Goblet, Dried Fruit, and Pretzels*.

Holland

The dramatic expression that flourished in Baroque Italy, France, Spain, and Flanders had been reinforced by the rejection of the Reformation and a reinvigoration of Catholicism. However, the Protestant world was looking in another direction, focusing on **landscapes** (pictures of scenery), still life compositions, and **genre painting** (scenes about everyday people and the natural world).

Young Woman with a Water-Jug by Jan Vermeer. Source: Metropolitan Museum of Art; Marquand Collection, Gift of Henry D. Marquand, 1889.

Rembrandt van Rijn became the most important artist in Amsterdam during this period. Although he was influenced by the drama and tenebrism of Caravaggio, he focused on the inner characteristics of a person or subject, whether it was religious or secular. He was a master draughtsman (illustrator of detailed, technical drawings), painter, and printmaker. He chose to work primarily in the medium of etching and is considered the greatest proponent of this process. He was a master storyteller in this format, sometimes inserting a sense of humor (as seen in his *Self-Portrait with a Cap*), and other times reflecting empathy and pathos, (as seen in his *The Hundred Guilder Print*).

By the 1640s, Rembrandt had also become a sought-after portrait painter. His portraits were mostly life-size and full-length and featured individuals or groups. Two of his most famous group paintings are *The Anatomy Lesson of Dr. Nicolae Tulp* and *The Night Watch*, which follow the Baroque style of capturing a moment in time and using light and shade to focus viewers' attention. His later works are remarkable for their psychological focus and introspective qualities. *Bathsheba with King David's Letter* emphasizes the subject's humanness and vulnerability.

Jan Vermeer is another artist of the period who represented the Dutch interest in everyday life. Rather than being focused on a dramatic scene, his pieces reflected the calm serenity of subjects performing everyday tasks seemingly deep in thought and enveloped in sense of privacy. His *Woman with a Water-Jug* and *Woman Holding a Balance* are two notable examples for his use of color and light.

ROCOCO AND NEOCLASSICISM

Rococo

As the **Enlightenment** (also known as the **Age of Reason**) developed in the eighteenth century, there was an even greater movement away from the dictates of church and state, and there was a progression toward rationality, scientific knowledge, and social equality. Remnants of the traditional world remained, but they were tempered by the changing social climate. Enlightened rulers still preferred beautiful things, but they had reservations about surrounding themselves with the symbols of grandeur and power that were prevalent in the Baroque period. The **Rococo** style tended to soften the weightiness of the Baroque period and emphasized a more lighthearted and delicate approach to creativity.

Decoration and Architecture

The Rococo style was first developed in France in the mid-1700s and represents the final phase of the Baroque period. Rococo began with a focus on interior decoration, and its goal was to delight the eye rather than send a message. Following the design trends associated with French royalty, **salons** (living rooms) were designed as the central place for the wealthy to receive guests and engage in intellectual discussions. These salons were characterized by elaborate ornamentation, curved and serpentine lines, and a pastel color palette. Furniture also became a medium for artistic craftsmanship, with mahogany used most often. Interior decorators came to be considered artists in their own right, along with the sculptors who created architectural ornamentation and the painters who decorated the ceilings and walls.

French furniture circa 1745–1749.
Source: Metropolitan Museum of Art; The Jack and Belle Linsky Collection, 1982.

Architecture reflected a lighter, more graceful style, emphasizing asymmetry and playfulness. In Germany and Austria, a new mood of exuberance led to much building in the Rococo style. The most important architect of the time was **Balthasar Neuman,** who oversaw the building of the **Basilika Vierzehnheiligen** Pilgrim Church (**Basilica of the Fourteen Holy Helpers**) and the **Residenz (Episcopal Palace)** in Würzberg. While the exteriors are relatively restrained, the interiors are overwhelmed with color, light, and decoration.

Painting

The overall impression of Rococo art is lightness, gaiety, and the pursuit of pleasure, with delicate ornamentation such as scrolls, ribbons, and gilt leaves and a pastel palette. The most representative Rococo painter in France was **Jean-Antoine Watteau,** who reflected a more Rubenesque style. He depicted classic themes that often revolved around youth and love and is noted for his soft dreamy atmospheres, as exemplified in his oil painting *Pilgrimage to Cythera.* **Frances Boucher** became a master of Rococo painting somewhat later. Although his work echoes some of the same characteristics of Watteau's, Boucher was slightly more suggestive and controversial, reflected in his *Blonde Odalisque,* which features a nude woman reclining. **Jean-Honoré Fragonard** is considered the last of the French Rococo painters. He would see all demand for Rococo style disappear with the French Revolution, but he epitomized the spirit of the Rococo style, with its dreaminess, soft colors, and dense landscape, in his painting *The Swing.*

The Swing by Jean-Honoré Fragonard. Source: National Gallery of Art.

In Austria and Southern Germany, Italian painting had the largest effect on the Rococo style. The Venetian painter **Giovanni Battista Tiepolo** painted frescoes for the Würzburg residence, as mentioned earlier. However, the most prominent painter of Bavarian Rococo churches was **Johann Baptist Zimmermann**, who painted the ceiling of the **Wieskirche**.

In England, eighteenth-century art reflected a hybrid style, blending Rococo color and light with a more naturalistic, less artificially perfect treatment. **Thomas Gainsborough** dominated portrait painting in England, using lush landscapes, relatively large figures, and simple and dignified poses.

Neoclassicism

As the appeal of Rococo began to decline, another style influenced artists in the eighteenth century. **Neoclassicism** corresponded naturally with the Enlightenment because it directly opposed the ornamentation, frivolity, and asymmetry of the Rococo style, preferring the clarity, simplicity, and intellectualism implied in the classical style. Neoclassicism emphasized straight lines, simple forms, minimal use of color, and close adherence to classical techniques. It encompassed all of the arts, but it was reflected most strongly in architecture, sculpture, and the decorative arts. At that time, the many discoveries of ancient-world artifacts provided numerous accessible examples for artists to imitate.

Architecture

The **Panthéon** in Paris, designed by **Jacques-Germain Soufflot**, reflects the Neoclassic style, using classic proportions in its columns and pediments. Neoclassicism also found a home in the United States, with architects like **Thomas Jefferson** and the historical landmark Monticello, and **Charles Bulfinch**, who designed the United States Capitol Building.

United States Capitol Building. Source: Library of Congress.

In England, Neoclassic architecture first appeared alongside the Baroque as a rebellion against its flamboyance. The first significant Neoclassic architect in England, **Inigo Jones**, observed classic symmetry and balance in his Banqueting House at Whitehall in London, with its simple design and windows separated by columns. **William Kent's** Chiswick House is another structure influenced by classic purity and simplicity. **Sir Christopher Wren**, responsible for renovating St. Paul's Cathedral, also adopted a Neoclassic style by creating a classical pedimented facade with tall bell towers that balanced the central dome. Later, the Neoclassic style would be continued with architects like **John Nash**, who designed Buckingham Palace.

Painting

Neoclassic painting was characterized by balancing emotion and restraint and by its echoing of the classic ideals of republican freedom and opposition to tyranny. **Anton Raphael Mengs**, who painted the ceiling fresco *Parnassus*, provided one of the first full expressions of Neoclassicism. However, **Jacques-Louis David** was the quintessential painter of the movement as exemplified by the *Oath of Horatii*, which is a combination of triangular composition and dramatic effect, and *The Death of Socrates*, which is a perfect statement of Neoclassical style.

The Death of Socrates by Jacques-Louis David. Source: The Metropolitan Museum of Art; Catharine Lorillard Wolfe Collection, Wolfe Fund, 1931.

Jean-August-Dominique Ingres was a follower of David's. His *Portrait of Monsieur Bertin* blends a straightforward depiction of the subject's imperfect physicality with Bertin's self-assured energy and determination. Ingres's painting of *La Grande Odalisque*, however, presented an idealized version of the feminine figure that some have claimed was a foreshadowing of a shift toward Romanticism.

Another Neoclassical painter, **Angelica Kauffman**, inspired many British artists to become history painters. Two of her famous works include *Cornelia Pointing to Her Children as Her Treasures*, which emphasizes the theme of the "good mother" and teaches a metaphorical lesson, and *The Artist in the Character of Design Listening to the Inspiration of Poetry*, which is an allegorical narrative depicting the artist as the Muse of Design.

One of the most successful British history painters was **Benjamin West**, who was also influenced by classic masters but bold enough to paint contemporary scenes such as *The Death of General Wolf*. Although it was despised by King George III because it defied convention by depicting contemporary uniforms, it was widely applauded by the public, who felt as though they were witnessing the death of a great national hero.

Another would-be history painter was **Joshua Reynolds**. Although he was forced to paint portraits to earn a living, he managed to fill them with classic references. One of his most famous paintings, *Lady Sarah Bunbury Sacrificing to the Graces*, displays the subject wearing what looks like classical drapery and an antique pedestal carrying a sculpture of The Three Graces.

Sculpture

The principal Neoclassical sculptors of the time were **Antonio Canova** and **Jean-Antoine Houdin**. One of Canova's most respected works is his *Psyche Revived by Cupid's Kiss*. Although it is sensual and erotic, it is classically symmetrical and restrained. This blend of simplicity and grace is also seen in his sculpture *Pauline Bonaparte Borghese as Venus Victorious*. Houdin is famous for his portrait busts and statues of philosophers, inventors, and figures of the Enlightenment. His subjects included Benjamin Franklin, Jean-Jacques Rousseau, Voltaire, Molière, George Washington, Thomas Jefferson, and Napoléon Bonaparte.

ROMANTICISM AND REALISM

Romanticism

The end of the eighteenth century and the beginning of the nineteenth century ushered in the Romantic movement in art. Countering the rational and restrained ideals of the Enlightenment, Romantics stressed that human senses and emotions were just as important as reason and order. The revolutions in France and America, which rejected rule by monarchy or religion, stressed the importance of human equality and individuality of thought. Romantic art also embraced an almost spiritual attachment to the natural world, rejecting the notion of absolute rules or standards.

Painting

Painting, rather than architecture or sculpture, seemed to most readily capture Romantic goals, as it was less restricted by standards or form. Spontaneity, sincerity, truthfulness, and the outpouring of emotion were first and foremost, and painting styles could be more fluid.

Francisco Goya was a close observer of the world around him, and he had very strong feelings about the ruthlessness of power and the arrogance of the social elite. In his painting *The Third of May*, he reveals the horrible execution of the Madrileños, a group of Madrid's citizens who had been guilty only of demonstrating against the Napoléon occupation. Another notable piece is Goya's portrait of *The Family of Charles IV*, which was painted at the height of his career as a Spanish court painter. In what first appears as an honoring portrait of the royal family, he slyly disguises his criticism with his blunt and grotesquely realistic portrayal.

In France, **Théodore Géricault** depicted dramatic scenes with an emphasis on emotion and atmosphere. His *Raft of Medusa* depicted a shipwreck in realistic and dramatic detail. Corpses slipped into the ocean at the bottom left of the composition, while there was commotion at the center, and a muscular survivor appeared at the top right waving his shirt to call for rescue. A more subtle painting in this dramatic style is *Evening: Landscape with an Aqueduct*, which emphasizes a stormy sky and the sublime power of nature.

Evening: Landscape with an Aqueduct by Théodore Géricault.
Source: Metropolitan Museum of Art; Purchase, Gift of James A. Moffet 2nd,
in memory of George M. Moffet, by exchange, 1989.

After Gericault died, his friend **Victor Delacroix** became the foremost representative of the Romantic movement with his emphasis on emotion and the dramatic and vivid portrayal of suffering. Delacroix is notable for his masterful use of expressive color and his depth of imagination. Like his mentor, he supported the liberal movements of his day and used his paintings to make a statement. Two of his most famous paintings are *The Massacre at Chios*, which is notable for his use of color to create form, and *The Death of Sardanapalus*, which blends reality with imaginative detail.

Landscape Art

The Romantic movement also encouraged the depiction of landscapes, reflecting the Romantic love of nature and the need to express one's personal experience with it. Two British artists are notable for their landscape art. The love of nature is obvious in paintings by **John Constable**, which were both subjective and based in reality. In his landscapes, such as *The Hay Wain* and *Wivenhoe Park, Essex*, he reflected both the realism of the scene and atmosphere he experienced.

Wivenhoe Park, Essex by John Constable. Source: National Gallery of Art.

Joseph Mallord William Turner strove for even greater subjectivity in his landscapes. Many of his scenes were filled with dynamic drama, reflecting the awesome power of nature and emphasizing the vulnerability of humanity. By stressing the intensity of consciousness, his work helped to define Romanticism while setting the stage for Impressionism. Two of his most famous works include *Dutch Boats in a Gale*, which emphasizes the ominous power of the sea, and *The Slave Ship*, which uses vibrant color to meld sky, fire, and water in a depiction of ailing slaves being thrown overboard as they sailed to be sold.

Caspar David Friedrich infused his landscapes with spiritual significance, believing that nature reflected the magnificence of God's presence in the world. His subdued color palette, sensitive depictions of misty atmospheres, and interplay of darkness and light reflected the dramatic power of nature, often making viewers feel empty and insignificant. Friedrich used **rückenfigur** in many of his paintings, a technique that depicts a person from behind viewing a scene. His most famous example is *Wanderer Above a Sea of Mist*.

In America, landscape painting eclipsed portraiture as the most esteemed art form by the 1840s. As Americans strived for their own identity, they looked to the abundance of unspoiled land around them for inspiration. **Thomas Cole** was famous for having brought European Romanticism to the United States. He believed that untamed nature best embodied God's spirit and that Americans were uniquely blessed. His painting, *The Oxbow*, represents his ideal of the wilderness being in harmony with cultivated fields and peaceful settlements. He stood against the rapid industrial and land development that was occurring during the Jacksonian era, and he worried that the natural destruction would lead to America's undoing.

Realism

Just as the Neoclassicists sought an artistic counterpart to reason, and the Romanticists emphasized feeling, intuition, and imagination, artists who subscribed to **Realism** were influenced primarily by science. They believed that facts mattered more than human feeling, and that **empiricism** (the observation of factual reality) was the foundation of knowledge. The here and now were more important than history and tradition, and contemporary and popular themes were most worthy of artistic expression.

France

French Realism developed alongside the Revolution of 1848, which occurred when the working class demanded more equal representation. It was a political movement, celebrating socialist ideals and condemning the aristocratic and bourgeois suppression of the working poor. It also emphasized the idea that traditional ideals and manners should be cast aside to make way for a new way of viewing the world.

One of the first French Realist artists was **Honoré Daumier**, a printer and caricaturist who used his work to criticize society and the government. His caricature *Le Ventre Legislatif* (*The Legislative Belly*) best underscores his disdain for political greed and corruption by depicting highly recognizable members of the Chamber of Deputies as bloated, bored, and ridiculous.

Gustave Courbet insisted on emphasizing the physical reality of what he observed, even if that reality was imperfect and ordinary. He gained notoriety by focusing on humble scenes and individuals, raising common experience to a level of importance never before seen. Courbet was also known for his portrayal of erotic, hedonistic, and matter-of-fact depictions. His *Burial at Ornans* is almost "anti-classic" in its frank portrayal of death as the end of life. There are no allusions to an afterlife, just the simple fact of a coffin being buried underground. His *A Young Woman Reading* depicts a simple, everyday event in an ordinary life, but is infused with a sexuality that was considered shocking at that time.

A Young Woman Reading by Gustave Courbet. Source: National Gallery of Art.

Edward Manet was one of the most influential artists who depicted modern life, often scandalizing the public with his disregard for convention by injecting unexpected images into his pieces and challenging accepted moral and aesthetic boundaries. His *Luncheon on the Grass* is a prime example, with its depiction of a naked woman sitting on the grass with two fully dressed men. Although he intentionally based the composition on classical works, the stiffness and flattened appearance of the subjects and disregard for scale accentuated his belief that artists needed to abandon the standards of the past and consider different approaches.

America

After the Civil War, the United States was being reshaped almost haphazardly as the population moved west and gained new territory. The new industrialized and expanded nation began to enjoy a different kind of prosperity, benefitting from scientific discovery, new inventions, and more time for leisure activities. American Realists celebrated these changes by emphasizing contemporary life with a wholesomeness that was entirely American.

Thomas Eakins reflected the modern world with a detailed accuracy that could almost be considered scientific in its approach. Eakins painted popular pastimes but also the newest scientific practices, such as anesthesia and antiseptic surgery. His images of sculling are widely known, as evidenced in *Max Schmitt in a Single Scull*, which celebrates the contemporary sports hero with precise perspective, lighting, and accurate detail.

Max Schmitt in a Single Scull by Thomas Eakins. Source: Metropolitan Museum of Art; Purchase, The Alfred N. Punnett Endowment Fund and George D. Pratt Gift, 1934.

Winslow Homer was another artist who depicted the leisure activities and ordinary moments in American life. Although his images used lighting and color in an almost impressionistic style, the figures were realistically solid and emotionally controlled, capturing scenes almost frozen in time. His *Snap the Whip*, which depicts barefoot country boys grasping hands and running across a field, accurately represented reality but revealed an optimism and hope for the future. Homer's unique realistic style evolved over time and was captured in many works, including illustrations, oil paintings, and watercolors. He is most famous for his ocean scenes, such as the scenes depicted in *Breezing Up*, which captures boys sailing in the wind, and in *The Fog Warning*, which captures a fisherman rowing alone and looking up at a threatening sky.

IMPRESSIONISM AND POST-IMPRESSIONISM

Impressionism

In the second half of the nineteenth century, a new generation of French painters created an art movement that rejected the established standards of the time. These painters strove to capture the fleeting, sensory effect of a real scene or event—the **impression** an artist perceived—rather than a linear and detailed depiction. They were inspired by the way that sunlight affected the perception of objects, noting that forms often dissolved into facets of color. They used fast, short, open brushstrokes to achieve this style, and they often worked outdoors *en plein air* (French for *in plain air*) in order to capture the light effects and atmosphere of a scene.

The most passionate follower of this movement was **Claude Monet**, whose dissolution of surfaces and separation of light into separate components of paint best exemplify the style. In his *Impression: Sunrise*, he used only small strokes of color to represent the view of the harbor of Le Havre as sailing vessels sailed toward the morning sun. Monet's diffused impressions of light and color and depictions of water and garden scenes continue to delight us to this day. His many notable works include *Rouen Cathedral, West Facade, Sunlight*, and his series of *Water Lilies*.

Working alongside Monet, **Pierre-August Renoir** also based his art primarily on optical impressions and the effects of light. However, he focused mostly on human figures and scenes depicting Parisian life. His *Le Moulin de la Galette* expresses all the loveliness and merriment of an afternoon dance. In *By the Seashore*, the softness of Impressionism, with its background composed of quick strokes, is combined with a more linear and careful handling of facial details.

By the Seashore by Pierre-August Renoir. Source: Metropolitan Museum of Art; H. O. Havemeyer Collection, Bequest of Mrs. H. O. Havemeyer, 1929.

Urban life was also captured by **Edgar Degas**, but his inclination toward realism and the use of linear curves and solid structures set him apart from other Impressionists who focused on color. He painted many pictures of women in movement, especially ballet dancers, and he was heavily influenced by the developing art of photography and Japanese woodcuts that were becoming readily available in Europe. *The Rehearsal* and *The Dancing Class* reflect this particularly, with their asymmetrical photographic composition, use of linear design, and sense of flatness rather than perspective.

The Dancing Class by Edgar Degas. Source: The Metropolitan Museum of Art; H. O. Havemeyer Collection, Bequest of Mrs. H. O. Havemeyer, 1929.

Berthe Morisot and **Mary Cassatt** were two leading figures of the Impressionist movement who focused on female subjects and subject matter. Two of Morisot's most famous works, *The Cradle* and *Interior*, are notable for their enigmatic depictions of modern women. In both cases, it is not clear what the subject is thinking, and the emotional expressions are complex. Morisot was also famous for boldly leaving some of her works looking unfinished, which pushed artistic boundaries.

Mary Cassatt was an American-born woman who was also part of the circle of Impressionists. She focused on women and women's issues as subjects, specializing in mother and child images. Like Degas, she was also influenced by Japanese art, and her paintings blend the light colors and loose brushstrokes of Impressionism with the flat planes and bold lines of that style. She is most notable for her *Little Girl in Blue Armchair*, which captures her perceptive observations of childhood, and *The Child's Bath*, which movingly depicts the intense emotional and physical involvement between a mother and child.

Camille Pissarro was an artist who worked in both the Impressionist and Post-Impressionist styles. His most notable works masterfully capture everyday rural life, as well as effects of light on color. He also stands out for his gentle nature and love of experimentation, which made him a mentor to many other artists. His *Hoar Frost, Old Road to Ennery, Pontoise,* and *Hay Harvest at Eragny* reflect his love of rural life, and his emphasis on color harmony and his focus on composition reflect movement toward a Post-Impressionist style.

Post-Impressionism

During the latter years of the nineteenth century, another group of artists drew together in rebellion against the fleeting impressions and disregard for composition that were hallmarks of the Impressionist style. Although they were united in moving away from Impressionism, their styles were far less unified. Post-Impressionists fell into two groups: one that focused on compositional structure and the effect of light on color and another that integrated line and color with symbolism.

Henri de Toulouse-Lautrec, who designed posters advertising the Moulin Rouge, elevated advertising to the status of fine art. As a child, Toulouse-Lautrec struggled with illness and disability, but he turned these struggles to his advantage, allowing him to see others without being noticed. His observations of people living on the margins of society made him an important visual historian of Parisian life. He focused on working-class individuals as his subjects. *The Streetwalker* depicts a prostitute sitting in a garden as a quite dignified individual, focusing on her distinctive features while visually hinting at her profession though her slight smile and confrontational pose. He is also famous for his poster, *Moulin Rouge: La Goulue*, which departs from his earlier Impressionist style by using large bands of color and strong outlines.

Georges Seurat was most notable for his painting *A Sunday Afternoon on the Island of La Grande Jatte*. While it echoes the Impressionist style, it is much more controlled in its rendering. The poised figures and idealistic scene are a far departure from the casual and spontaneous sensations that the Impressionists favored.

Although he originally followed the Impressionists' use of color and subject matter, **Paul Cézanne** moved toward a more analytic, almost sculptural style. He is credited with linking the temporary aspects of Impressionism with a sense of the permanent, paving the way for the later styles of

Fauvism, Cubism, and Expressionism. He accentuated the solidity of his subjects by using simple forms and color planes that were almost geometrically perceived. His *Still Life with a Basket of Apples* and his *Still Life with Apples and a Pot of Primroses* are not so much reflections of real objects in real space as representations of multiple perspectives at the same time. His *Mont Sainte-Victoire*, one of a series of paintings of the same scene, is another piece that depicted a solid and essential reality. As Cézanne's art became more abstract, he gave future artists the permission to make art less representational and more inventive.

Still Life with Apples and a Pot of Primroses by Paul Cézanne.
Source: Metropolitan Museum of Art; Bequest of Sam A. Lewisohn, 1951.

Vincent van Gogh intensely desired a meaningful life and believed that art could give him access to an ideal world. His paintings were filled with emotion, color, and vibrancy, and he painted as if he were trying to explain the world as he saw it. In *Starry Night*, he painted far more from imagination than nature and infused the scene with what he felt, rather than what he saw. The swirling forms and brilliant colors are presented in multidirectional strokes of **impasto** (thick applications of paint) that are reflective of the range of his emotions from joy and hope to anxiety and despair. He imbued each of his paintings with a spiritual and psychological tone, and his brushstrokes closely reflected his feelings at the time. His *Cypresses* was also painted in a similar style.

Cypresses by Vincent van Gogh. Source: Metropolitan Museum of Art; Rogers Fund, 1949.

Paul Gaugin also wanted to express his feelings through art, and he used broad areas of intense color, symbolism, and bold black outlines to do so. He called his style **synthetism** because he believed it synthesized observation and impression. His *Mahana No Atua* (*Day of the God*) exemplifies this approach with its blending of actual and symbolic details.

Symbolism

Gaugin's and van Gogh's art came to be known as **Symbolism**, a movement that focused on a subjective interpretation of reality rather than detached observation. Symbolism pushed the everyday world aside, and artists focused on their inner dreams, deep-seated fears, and desires. The goal of penetrating psychological interpretation is evident in the sculptures of **August Rodin**. *The Thinker* represented the hopelessness and futility of life, and the *Burghers of Calais* highlighted the sacrifices they endured rather than their reputations as heroes. Instead of carefully smoothing his pieces, Rodin presented his figures as rough and almost unfinished to symbolize the temporary existence of modern humanity.

Art Nouveau

The Art Nouveau movement, which appeared at the turn of the twentieth century, grew from a desire to move beyond the previous focus on traditional subjects toward a celebration of the modern world. At this time, industrialization had become widespread, and many decorative works were poorly made and easily duplicated.

The **Art Nouveau** artists were inspired by both organic and geometric forms, and they advocated the notion that art could be represented through useful, everyday objects. Their works applauded new technologies like telephones, electric lights, and furniture. Architecture was also heavily influenced by this move toward modernism. One of the strangest creations of the time derived from the imagination of **Antoni Gaudi**. The **Casa Mila Apartments** in Barcelona evokes Spanish Baroque and Renaissance architecture but has an undulating and irregular "sandy" appearance that strongly reflects Barcelona's connection to the sea.

EARLY TWENTIETH CENTURY

The early twentieth century saw new ways of experiencing and understanding the world that developed from the art and culture that preceded it. Abstraction, symbolism, and the unique perceptions of the artist became first and foremost. There was a belief that humans experienced life as disparate memories and observations that they needed to coalesce into ideas. Artists completely broke away from traditional styles and focused on an almost scientific approach that embraced new ideas and perceptual frontiers.

Emergence of Modernism

Some modern artists focused on new models of visual perception, while others sought to capture the technology of the contemporary world. Still others pursued a more spiritual and abstract understanding of the new civilization they encountered.

Fauvism

The first major style to emerge developed from the styles of van Gogh and Gaugin. Fauvists used color to express their emotions but went beyond to use color and linear patterns more boldly, almost harshly, to defy traditional approaches and create a more direct reflection of their experience. Their art skewed perspectives and borrowed the styles of nontraditional ancient cultures.

Henri Matisse pushed the use of color as a structural element and went on to suspend logical space and scale in this work. Reality gave way to expression, and a flatness and two-dimensionality underscored his approach. He also strove to present an optimistic view of life, using color and line to achieve this effect, even with his representations of the human figure. The portrait of Matisse's wife, *The Woman with a Hat*, is an example of his modernistic approach, with its bold departure from conventional portraiture and his wild use of color throughout the piece. Another example of his style is *Laurette in a Green Robe*, which presents the subject as angular and highly abstract.

Expressionism

This artistic movement stressed a departure from realism and placed an emphasis on the inner, mostly turbulent, emotions of the artist. It strongly echoed the works of van Gogh and Gaugin, but focused more on the darker preoccupations of fear, death, and loneliness. *The Scream*, by Edvard Munch, best exemplifies this focus on pain and isolation by reflecting a society he perceived to be desensitized.

The mood of isolation and fear was also captured by **Ernst Ludwig Kirchner**, who represented the German Expressionists who called themselves **Die Brüke (The Bridge)**. In his painting *Street, Dresden*, he suggested loneliness and uncertainty with his feverish brushwork and odd color schemes. His *Dance Hall Bellevue* evoked energy and life.

Dance Hall Bellevue by Ernst Ludwig Kirschner. Source: National Gallery of Art.

Wassily Kandinsky, who was a member of a second German Expressionist group called **Der Blaue Reiter** (**The Blue Rider**), moved even further toward **abstraction**—completely removed from a depiction of reality—to emphasize the artist's innermost concerns. His *Sketch I for Composition VII* is a prime example.

Cubism

Over history, art has always expressed the polarities between the emotions and the intellect. Fauvism and Expressionism emphasized emotion; however, **Cubism** emphasized intellectual analysis. **Pablo Picasso** was the foremost figure in this movement, with his abstract and geometric treatments of subjects. He once said, "I paint objects as I think them, not as I see them."

During what was known as his **Blue Period**, Picasso focused on melancholy figures who were downtrodden and trapped in their loneliness. *The Old Guitarist* exemplifies this, with its blue tonalities and its distorted representation of the human figure emphasizing the ghost-like and somber appearance of the subject. His style evolved with the portrait of *Gertrude Stein*, which also emphasizes simple shapes and flat planes but includes a sculptural effect. *Les Demoiselles d'Avignon* is a representation of Picasso's movement toward cubism, in which he echoes Cézanne's manipulation of space, achieving a flatness or two-dimensionality, as well as a representation of multiple viewpoints at once.

With **Georges Braque**, Picasso went on to fully develop **Cubism**, which completely deconstructed the notion of perspective, breaking up images into geometrical pieces that completely broke away from a depiction of reality. Abstraction became complete, with geometrical lines and curves only suggesting reality. Braque's *The Portuguese* and *Candlestick and Playing Cards on a Table* were prime examples of **Analytic Cubism**, consisting of only shapes that resembled architectural forms. Picasso's later works featured **collage** (composing a piece of art using preexisting materials) and would come to be known as **Synthetic Cubism**, as exemplified in *La Bouteille de Suze*, which is a combination of pasted paper, **gouache** (opaque pigments thickened with a glue-like substance), and charcoal.

Futurism

The **Futurism** movement started a few years after the beginning of Cubism under the leadership of poet Filippo Marinetti. His manifesto called for art that was violent, energetic, bold, and free from the boundaries of harmony and good taste. Umberto Boccioni's sculpture, *Unique Forms of Continuity,* is a prime example of this movement. It communicates the energy of movement, but there are no representative details.

Unique Forms of Continuity in Space by Umberto Boccioni.
Source: Metropolitan Museum of Art; Bequest of Lydia Winston Malbin, 1989.

Art Between the World Wars

The period between World War I and World War II has been characterized as a time of disillusionment. People tried to find meaning in a world that had dramatically changed with the arrival of technological advances. The competing ideologies of democracy, anarchy, socialism, and fascism strove for supremacy, and countries vied for territory and influence. Competing notions about what would bring about human happiness also ranged from the hedonism of the Jazz Age to the quest for utopias that would bring equality and prosperity to everyone. Similarly, the visual arts evolved in many different ways between 1914 and 1945. The continuing development of abstract art, realism, and architecture would pull the world in many different directions.

De Stijl

In Russia and western Europe, art was dedicated to complete abstraction and nonobjective expression. The **De Stijl** movement, also known as **Neo-Plasticism**, was different from Cubism in that it was a complete departure from nature. Compositions consisted mostly of strong black lines, primary colors, and geometric shapes. The *Composition No. II/Composition I/Composition with Red, Blue, and Yellow* by **Piet Mondrian** are examples from this movement.

Dada

In 1916, during World War I, an international movement arose that insisted that art have no meaning because the world was absurd. Works that were created during this period were imbued with nihilism, were nonsensical and randomly composed, and were full of irreverence. **Marcel Duchamp** was a champion of the movement, with his *Fountain*, which is nothing more than a urinal turned upside down. He challenged the notion of technique or talent and focused on art as a manifestation of ideas.

Surrealism

Surrealism was defined by a manifesto that declared that art was meant to reflect unfettered thought, irrational and outside of any moral or aesthetic standards. Surrealists believed in a complete exploration of the unconscious, that true reality went beyond the superficial appearance of things. There were two branches of this philosophy: **illusionistic surrealism**, which created art that expressed a kind of dream state, and **automatic surrealism**, which represented a spontaneous outpouring of the unconscious mind.

Artist **Salvador Dali** worked in the illusionistic surrealism style, creating images from real life that were bizarrely shaped and visually dreamlike, provoking viewers to explore their subconscious. In *The Persistence of Memory*, Dali portrayed melting watches and swarming ants that suggested decay. He purposely used images that were metaphors for the mind's deepest desires and fears.

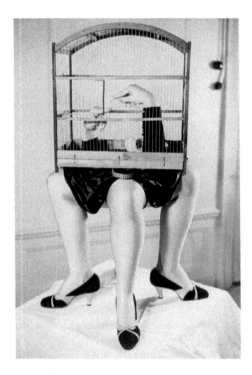

Surrealistic art, *l'Ultrameuble* by Kurt Seligmann (anonymous, 1938).
Source: Rijksmuseum.nl.

Joan Miró believed that introspective subject matter was likely to be meaningless to the observer. He preferred the automatist surrealism style, painting spontaneous shapes and colors to be aesthetically pleasing. His *Painting, 1933* depicts clusters of organic images that float in space and reflect nothing from the real world. *Composition* is another piece in the same style but more suggestive of creatures and spirits.

The Bauhaus

Most of the Dadaist, Surrealist, and abstract artists of the time favored socialism and rejected the materialism brought about by modern society. They advocated social progress for the working class and believed that their art would inspire change. However, it was the **Bauhaus School** that arose as the strongest advocate for social progress. The Bauhaus, meaning "House of Building," was dedicated to blending the fine and applied arts using manufacturing to create practical, everyday products, such as chairs and textiles.

Architecture and interior design were once again considered works of art. *The Club Chair (Model B3, also called The Wassily Chair)*, designed by **Marcel Breuer**, is representative of this movement. Lightweight and easily mass-produced, its stainless-steel tubes and fabric panels epitomize the Bauhaus philosophy. Bauhaus architecture is best exemplified in the **Bauhaus Building** in Dessau, Germany. Its clean, rectangular shape; glass walls; and vertical logo became synonymous with what we now think of as modern style.

Social Realism

Artists during this period also sought to draw social and political attention to the realities that common people were facing, especially the tension between the haves and have-nots. Artists created works to portray common people as heroic figures, inspiring sympathy and spurring social change.

One of the offshoots of this movement was the **Harlem Renaissance** of the 1920s and 1930s, which called attention to the realities of African Americans and their quest for equality and dignity. **Jacob Lawrence** painted *The Life of Harriet Tubman, No. 4, 1939–1940* to celebrate the African American identity and history of his people's struggle for freedom. He was also known for his Cubist style, and the abstractions in his *Migration* series made powerful and inspirational statements about the possibilities for a better life.

In the Midwest, a group of artists preferred to work with **figurative art** (realistic representations) to draw attention to the hardworking and religious descendants of the pioneers in America. *American Gothic* by **Grant Wood** became one of the most well-known and iconic images of stoicism and serenity. Photographer **Dorothea Lange** captured the destitution of migrant famers, and her image of *Migrant Mother, California* so powerfully captured their plight that the government immediately took action to send food and open relief camps.

Edward Hopper was another artist who embraced realistic expression, evidenced in his paintings *Nighthawks* and *Ground Swell*.

Ground Swell by Edward Hopper. Source: National Gallery of Art; Corcoran Collection.

Frida Kahlo was a Mexican painter who created self-portraits to depict the human suffering that many of her people faced. Her *Diego in My Thoughts* is painted in a surrealistic style and highlights the artist's fervent wish to conquer death. **Diego Rivera** was another Mexican painter, famous for his fresco murals that feature Mexican traditions and celebrated the indigenous culture of his people. Rivera painted his *Distributing Arms* in what he believed was an ancient Mayan technique, emphasizing the heroism and triumph of the Mexican Revolution.

POSTWAR TO POSTMODERN

The decades that followed World War II saw the United States emerge as the leading economic power in the world. The Atomic Age had begun, and the realization that human beings could be annihilated brought about international tensions and a general air of foreboding. At the same time, however, the global economy was taking root, creating a delicate economic, social, and political network. The philosophy that dominated at this time was **existentialism**, which focused on self-examination and the importance of individuals finding meaning for themselves.

Abstract Expressionism

Existentialism emphasized the notion that there were no absolute truths, and artists insisted that all that mattered was a subjective view of the world. Any symbols or references to the natural world dissolved, and **Abstract**

Expressionism thrived. Paintings emphasized spontaneity, action, and intense color.

Jackson Pollock was the foremost representative of this movement. He applied paint by dripping, throwing, and splattering huge canvases without any regard for the edges of the surface, creating an illusion of infinity. Pollock created *Autumn Rhythm (Number 30)* by allowing his unconscious to control his actions as if he were in thrall to his own basic impulses. When asked if the painting had any meaning, he said that "any attempt on my part to say something about it. . . could only destroy it."

The action painter who influenced future Abstract artists was **Willem de Kooning**. Like Pollock, he created his paintings through powerful gestures that came from his feelings, but he imposed a Cubist structure with overlapping planes of color and severe, jagged lines. His *Woman I* depicts a collection of feminine shapes that project an angry and powerful mood, as though the artist was trying to express his distaste for women—although he insisted that the piece was meant to be comical.

Formalist Abstraction

Formalist Abstraction, also known as **Hard-Edge Abstraction** developed as an alternative to Abstract Expressionism. Rejecting the bold-action brushwork of Pollock and Kooning, formalist painters sought to make unemotional art by painting exact, smooth planes, and accentuating the flatness of the canvas. **Ellsworth Kelly** was a proponent of this movement that brought a stark simplicity to painting. In his *Red Blue Green*, he used just three geometric shapes in bold colors to represent nothing, but there is a sense of movement implied by the interaction of the colors and shapes.

Another type of formalist abstraction, called **Color Stain Painting**, was represented by the artwork of **Helen Frankenthaler**. Her painting, *The Bay*, exemplifies this style with her complete avoidance of brushwork. By literally pouring paint on a canvas, she created a sensuous and attractive surface, blending the image and the canvas as one.

Another group of artists emphasized **Minimalism**, reducing their ideas to the simplest forms and using the fewest colors and textures. **Joseph Stella** simply repeated basic lines in geometric patterns using one single color in his *Mas o Menos (More or Less)*. There is a controlled, sculptural feeling to this abstract piece, and no is emotion expressed. It is far removed from the Abstract Expressionism exemplified by Pollock and Kooning.

Pop Art: A Rejection of Abstract Expressionism

Pop art derived its name from its focus on popular culture. Pop artists reproduced mundane subjects from the real world, mainly mass media, at times lifting the mundane to the status of fine art. Andy Warhol and Roy Lichtenstein were the most famous pop artists. **Andy Warhol** is well-known for his reproductions of soup cans and celebrity portraits that are presented as common, bland aspects of contemporary life. His most famous works are *32 Campbell Soup Cans, Green Coca-Cola Bottles,* and *Shot Marilyns* (portraits of Marilyn Monroe with different color backgrounds). **Roy Lichtenstein** is notable for his paintings of comic-book scenes, which accentuated the kinds of dot patterns used in printing to create light and shade. His famous *Drowning Girl* is hanging in the Museum of Modern Art.

Jasper Johns is most famous for his painting *Three Flags*, which depicts three different-sized American flags, one on top of the other. While no real meaning can be implied from the piece, it was deliberately and carefully created as art, inviting the viewer to focus on the way the painting was made rather than why. **Robert Rauschenberg** is notable for his **combine paintings** (attaching various everyday items to the canvas), such as *Bed*, which combines paint, pencil, a pillow, sheet, and quilt on wood supports.

Post-Minimalism

By the mid-1960s, art once again moved in a different direction, this time abandoning the emotionless representations of earlier Abstract art. Artists who dominated this movement were determined to promote the rights of people who had been overlooked by previous artistic movements. Post-minimalism artists wanted to use their art to make statements about what they felt and believed. They placed ideas first and foremost.

Conceptual Art is based entirely on an idea—apart from aesthetics. Some conceptual art existed only as words. The idea could also be manifested as a graph, chart, map, or photograph. **Joseph Kosuth** was a leading figure in this movement, most notable for his exposition *One and Three Chairs*, which presents a wooden folding chair, a photographic copy of the chair, and an enlargement of a dictionary definition of the chair. His goal was simply to convey the concept of "chairness."

Site-Specific Art

By the late sixties, artists moved beyond canvases and galleries, sculpting with earth and snow and depicting geological and other weather events in photographs and drawings. **Robert Smithson** created one of the most famous earthworks (works created by changing the natural environment). His *Spiral Jetty* involved moving tons of mud and black basalt and is located at a remote area of Utah's Great Salt Lake. The spiral shape accumulates salt on its sides, making the color of the water in the interior of the form change to an almost red color. The fact that the jetty will eventually disappear into the lake is part of the artist's point.

Art with a Social Agenda

Most of the postwar artists up to this time stayed away from social commentary or hid it so that it was not obvious. **Judy Chicago** strongly promoted **feminist** causes with her artwork and educational art studio at Fresno State College. *The Dinner Party* is a multimedia work made of painted porcelain, textile, and needlework that celebrates historically significant women and their accomplishments. Photographer **Robert Mapplethorpe** created black-and-white images that honored people who were criticized by society for their sexual identity and unconventional sexual proclivities. **Romare Bearden** became famous for his collages celebrating African American culture. Two of his most notable works are *The Dove* and *The Prevalence of Ritual: Baptism*, which synthesize Cubism and Abstract Expressionism.

CONTEMPORARY

The Postmodern Era: Art Since 1980

By 1980, the art world determined that the context of a work of art was critical to a full understanding of it. In other words, a Renaissance painting was likely to have meant something completely different to a person living at that time, in contrast to the person viewing it today. Similarly, at this point, artists felt strongly that their art did not have to build upon the movements that had preceded it. Artists could express themselves in a multitude of styles and new media, including photography, electric signs, and video, without worrying about meeting specific evaluation standards.

The art establishment had also widened its traditional boundaries to include creators of all different ethnicities, races, cultures, and beliefs—without valuing one body of work over another. The globalization that had begun after World War II was now complete. Televisions, computers, cell phones, and satellites now connected artists from all over the world.

Architecture

After World War II, architecture moved in many different directions. Technological advances allowed skyscrapers and more sculptural building forms, and Classical standards were rejected in favor of innovative forms of expression. **Frank Lloyd Wright** was one of the most influential architects of the twentieth century. Wright strove to create buildings that were highly functional, while also organically blending them with their natural environment. **The Solomon R. Guggenheim Museum**, located in New York City, reflects a summary of Wright's functional goals. The flow of space is accentuated through curved walls, and there are very few interior partitions to obstruct a visitor's view.

A comparison of Wright's Guggenheim Museum in New York with its sister **Guggenheim Museum** in Bilbao, Spain, which was designed and built by **Frank Gehry**, exemplifies the architectural diversity that has since taken place. In this building, the architect was completely free of restrictions, creating a sculptural display of unique forms that were meant more as a symbolic statement. This building represented a new image for its city and turned it into a tourist destination.

Pluralism

During the 1980s, the idea of pluralism and limitless possibilities began to gain widespread acceptance. The last few decades have seen an abundance of creations in painting, photography, and video as the leading media.

Painting returned by the 1980s. In the previous two decades it had not disappeared, but it had been overshadowed by other types of art. The new type of painting that developed was called **Neo-Expressionism** because it had revived painting that echoed the Romanticism and Expressionism of the past. Two artists most notable in this movement are Anselm Kiefer from Germany and Jean-Michel Basquiat of the United States.

Anselm Kiefer is famous for focusing on German history and myth, particularly as it related to Nazism. His pieces incorporated the thick layering of paint (**impasto**) with materials such as lead, glass, dried flowers, and hay. *Dein Goldenes Haar, Margarethe* (*Your Golden Hair, Margarete*) depict a vast, yellow wasteland with a German tank at its center. The stick-like figure of Margarete is shedding strands of yellow hair, while at the top of the painting darker, incinerated hair is displayed in the distance.

Jean-Michel Basquiat was born of Haitian and Puerto Rican parents and had become a prolific painter by his early twenties, before he died of an overdose at age 27. Basquiat worked in a dynamic stream-of-consciousness style, combining painting, drawing, paper, and text into layers to stress messages about politics and racial identity. His *Horn Players*, which celebrates African American jazz musicians, is an excellent example of his style.

Video Art

Video art also emerged as a leading medium after the dawn of television, particularly after the introduction of wireless broadcasting and cable. Most notable for his sound and video installations is **Bill Viola**. Although some of his works do not have a clear narrative, there is always an existential questioning of the meaning of existence. *The Crossing*, which consists of two simultaneously presented videos with overwhelming sound effects, shows the same man approaching from a distance to fill the scene. In one video, the figure of the man bursts into flame, and in the other, he is deluged with water, disappearing into nothingness at the end of both videos. The work is a powerful sensory experience, leaving the viewer to ponder the fragility of existence and, some have suggested, the spiritual serenity of oblivion.

CONCLUSION

The variety of contemporary art and its many directions may leave us wondering about what is next. It seems as if we cannot ignore the past, but we also need to see life as it exists today. In a time when more people across the world have access to the creative works of others, it may help to recognize the duality of human existence—we are the same and we are different.

SUMMING IT UP

- Art origins in the **Ancient World** can be traced to the ancient regions and cultures found in the near East, Egypt, Greece, and Rome.
- **Sumerians** developed the first written symbols (**cuniform**), built temples to honor their gods, and created **steles** (upright marker stones carved in relief).
- The **Egyptian** devotion to the pharaoh is evidenced in the art found within the elaborate stepped pyramids and tombs. Artists used **hieroglyphics** in writings, paintings, reliefs, and colossal sculptures and tombs. They also employed a **composite view** technique, where rich, deep colors are used to present a profile or side view of people or animals.
- **Ancient Greek art** is notable for its naturalistic yet idealized representations of the human body, as well as its development of architectural forms. Colorful **frescoes**, geometric designs, and the first **Doric** and **Ionic** architectural styles came from this time.
- **Early Roman art and architecture** derived from its Etruscan heritage (temples, stone arches, terracotta statuary, multi-chambered frescoed tombs, and bronze objects and sculpture) but also had a heavy Greek influence. Early free-standing **stone busts** incorporated distinct facial features; later works incorporated a more idealistic style. Buildings were initially made with marble; concrete was used later to construct **barrel vaults**, **groin vaults**, and **hemispheric domes**.
- The **high and late Roman empires** saw the creation of **forums**, with the **Pantheon** as a prime example showcasing a vast **rotunda**. Mosaics were extensively used throughout these periods, imperial statues and funerary sculpture abounded, and relief sculpture became even more prominent.
- In the early **Christian period of the Middle Ages**, artists decorated **catacomb** walls and ceilings with frescoes and decorated **sarcophagi** (stone coffins) with a mix of Old and New Testament themes. Art was symbolistic and metaphorical to be ambiguous and recognizable only to Christians.
- Early **Byzantine** art and architecture of the Middle Ages focused on religious expression and primarily used mosaics and **icons** to convey Orthodox Christian beliefs. Usually created with **encaustic** (heated wax) paint, these works of art were meant to inspire believers, using a symbolic rather than a naturalistic perspective. Ivory carving and manuscript **illumination** were also important forms of art during this era.
- Hundreds of new churches and monasteries were built in Europe in the **Romanesque** period (1050–1200 CE) to celebrate the primacy of the Christian faith. One of the most famous examples is the **Cathedral of Pisa**, known for its leaning tower.

- The **Gothic** style of architecture developed in France in the middle of the twelfth century. It departed from the Romanesque style with its soaring pointed arches, thin walls, and huge stained-glass windows that lighted the interiors. The creation of the flying **buttress** enabled ceilings to be built without reinforcement. The **Notre Dame Cathedral** is a prime example of the Gothic style.
- The **Renaissance**, meaning "rebirth," is considered the artistic and intellectual link between the Middle Ages and contemporary times.
    - The fourteenth century ushered in a renewed focus on **humanism** as well as a shift from Byzantine spirituality to a focus on the natural world and its beauty.
    - Fifteenth-century Italian art includes **Lorenzo Ghiberti's** bronze doors known as the *Gate of Paradise*, **Brunelleschi's** dome of the Florence Cathedral, **Donatello's** *David*, and **Masaccio's** fresco paintings. Northern European art stressed the idea that individuals were free and that human beings could think for themselves, which ultimately led the way to the Reformation.
    - Three notable Italian artists emerged in the sixteenth century— **Leonardi da Vinci**, **Raphael**, and **Michelangelo**. The **mannerism** style materialized, characterized by the distortion of figures; flat, almost two-dimensional spaces; lack of a geometric focal point; and a jarring combination of colors.
- The **Baroque** style was born during the seventeenth century, combining Renaissance classicism with an exuberant theatricality, complexity, and opulence. The goal was to deliver a message of **absolutism** and unlimited grandeur to inspire followers to remain faithful to the Church.
- As the **Enlightenment** (also known as the **Age of Reason**) developed in the eighteenth century, there was an even greater movement away from the dictates of church and state, and a progression toward rationality, scientific knowledge, and social equality.
- The **Rococo** style sought to soften the weightiness of the Baroque period and emphasized a more lighthearted and delicate approach to creativity.
- **Neoclassicism** directly opposed the ornamentation, frivolity, and asymmetry of the Rococo style, preferring the clarity, simplicity, and intellectualism implied in the classical style. This movement emphasized straight lines, simple forms, minimal use of color, and close adherence to classical techniques.

- The end of the eighteenth century and the beginning of the nineteenth century ushered in the **Romantic** movement. Countering the rational and restrained ideals of the Enlightenment, Romantics stressed that human senses and emotions were just as important as reason and order. This movement embraced an almost spiritual attachment to the natural world, rejecting the notion of absolute rules or standards.
- Artists who subscribed to **Realism** were influenced primarily by science. Facts mattered more than human feeling, and **empiricism** (the observation of factual reality) was the foundation of knowledge. The here and now was more important than history and tradition, and contemporary and popular themes were most worthy of artistic expression.
- **Impressionism** developed in the second half of the nineteenth century. Painters strove to capture their impression of the fleeting, sensory effect of a real scene or event rather than a linear and detailed depiction. **Claude Monet, Pierre-August Renoir** and **Edgar Degas** are well-known impressionistic artists.
- **Post-Impressionists** fell into two groups: one that focused on compositional structure and the effect of light on color and another that integrated line and color with symbolism. Notable artists include **Henri de Toulouse-Lautrec, Paul Cézanne,** and **Vincent van Gogh.**
- The early twentieth century saw new ways of experiencing and understanding the world that developed from the art and culture that preceded it. This time period saw the emergence of **Modernism**, including Fauvism, Expressionism, Cubism, Futurism.
- Art between World War I and II is characterized as a time of disillusionment. The continuing development of abstract art, realism, and architecture would pull the world in many different directions. Art movements include **De Stijl** (also known as **Neo-Plasticism**), **Dada, Surrealism, Bauhaus,** and **Social Realism.**
- **Existentialism** dominated in the postwar to postmodern time. This philosophy emphasized the notion that there were no absolute truths, and artists insisted that a subjective view of the world was all that mattered. Any symbols or references to the natural world dissolved, and **Abstract Expressionism** thrived. Paintings emphasized spontaneity, action, and intense color.
- **Formalist Abstraction**, also known as **Hard-Edge Abstraction**, developed as an alternative to Abstract Expressionism. Formalist painters sought to make unemotional art by painting exact, smooth planes, and accentuating the flatness of the canvas.

- **Pop art** derived its name from its focus on popular culture. Pop artists reproduced mundane subjects from the real world, mainly mass media, at times lifting the mundane to the status of fine art. **Andy Warhol** is the most well-known pop artist.
- The **Post-Minimalism** movement in the mid-to-late 1960s was dominated by artists who were determined to promote the rights of people who had been overlooked by previous artistic movements. Post-minimalism artists wanted to use their art to make statements about what they felt and believed. They placed ideas first and foremost.
- **Contemporary** art is defined as art since 1980. Artists express themselves in a multitude of styles and media. Traditional boundaries have extended to include creators of all different ethnicities, races, cultures, and beliefs—without valuing one body of work over another. Advances in technology and globalization now connect artists from all over the world.

Chapter 4

Art of the Western World Post-Test

POST-TEST ANSWER SHEET

1. Ⓐ Ⓑ Ⓒ Ⓓ
2. Ⓐ Ⓑ Ⓒ Ⓓ
3. Ⓐ Ⓑ Ⓒ Ⓓ
4. Ⓐ Ⓑ Ⓒ Ⓓ
5. Ⓐ Ⓑ Ⓒ Ⓓ
6. Ⓐ Ⓑ Ⓒ Ⓓ
7. Ⓐ Ⓑ Ⓒ Ⓓ
8. Ⓐ Ⓑ Ⓒ Ⓓ
9. Ⓐ Ⓑ Ⓒ Ⓓ
10. Ⓐ Ⓑ Ⓒ Ⓓ
11. Ⓐ Ⓑ Ⓒ Ⓓ
12. Ⓐ Ⓑ Ⓒ Ⓓ
13. Ⓐ Ⓑ Ⓒ Ⓓ
14. Ⓐ Ⓑ Ⓒ Ⓓ
15. Ⓐ Ⓑ Ⓒ Ⓓ
16. Ⓐ Ⓑ Ⓒ Ⓓ

17. Ⓐ Ⓑ Ⓒ Ⓓ
18. Ⓐ Ⓑ Ⓒ Ⓓ
19. Ⓐ Ⓑ Ⓒ Ⓓ
20. Ⓐ Ⓑ Ⓒ Ⓓ
21. Ⓐ Ⓑ Ⓒ Ⓓ
22. Ⓐ Ⓑ Ⓒ Ⓓ
23. Ⓐ Ⓑ Ⓒ Ⓓ
24. Ⓐ Ⓑ Ⓒ Ⓓ
25. Ⓐ Ⓑ Ⓒ Ⓓ
26. Ⓐ Ⓑ Ⓒ Ⓓ
27. Ⓐ Ⓑ Ⓒ Ⓓ
28. Ⓐ Ⓑ Ⓒ Ⓓ
29. Ⓐ Ⓑ Ⓒ Ⓓ
30. Ⓐ Ⓑ Ⓒ Ⓓ
31. Ⓐ Ⓑ Ⓒ Ⓓ
32. Ⓐ Ⓑ Ⓒ Ⓓ

33. Ⓐ Ⓑ Ⓒ Ⓓ
34. Ⓐ Ⓑ Ⓒ Ⓓ
35. Ⓐ Ⓑ Ⓒ Ⓓ
36. Ⓐ Ⓑ Ⓒ Ⓓ
37. Ⓐ Ⓑ Ⓒ Ⓓ
38. Ⓐ Ⓑ Ⓒ Ⓓ
39. Ⓐ Ⓑ Ⓒ Ⓓ
40. Ⓐ Ⓑ Ⓒ Ⓓ
41. Ⓐ Ⓑ Ⓒ Ⓓ
42. Ⓐ Ⓑ Ⓒ Ⓓ
43. Ⓐ Ⓑ Ⓒ Ⓓ
44. Ⓐ Ⓑ Ⓒ Ⓓ
45. Ⓐ Ⓑ Ⓒ Ⓓ
46. Ⓐ Ⓑ Ⓒ Ⓓ
47. Ⓐ Ⓑ Ⓒ Ⓓ
48. Ⓐ Ⓑ Ⓒ Ⓓ

49. Ⓐ Ⓑ Ⓒ Ⓓ   **53.** Ⓐ Ⓑ Ⓒ Ⓓ   **57.** Ⓐ Ⓑ Ⓒ Ⓓ

50. Ⓐ Ⓑ Ⓒ Ⓓ   **54.** Ⓐ Ⓑ Ⓒ Ⓓ   **58.** Ⓐ Ⓑ Ⓒ Ⓓ

51. Ⓐ Ⓑ Ⓒ Ⓓ   **55.** Ⓐ Ⓑ Ⓒ Ⓓ   **59.** Ⓐ Ⓑ Ⓒ Ⓓ

52. Ⓐ Ⓑ Ⓒ Ⓓ   **56.** Ⓐ Ⓑ Ⓒ Ⓓ   **60.** Ⓐ Ⓑ Ⓒ Ⓓ

ART OF THE WESTERN WORLD POST-TEST

72 minutes—60 questions

Directions: Carefully read each of the following 60 questions. Choose the best answer to each question and fill in the corresponding circle on the answer sheet. The Answer Key and Explanations can be found following this post-test.

---

1. Which of the following painters is famous for rendering *The Rape of the Sabine Women?*

   A. Peter Paul Rubens
   B. Anthony Van Dyck
   C. Nicholas Poussin
   D. George de La Tour

2. Which of the following is a *ziggurat?*

   A. An upright marker
   B. A stepped pyramid
   C. A stepped tower
   D. An amphitheater

3. The Gothic style of architecture developed in which of the following countries?

   A. Germany
   B. Italy
   C. England
   D. France

4. Which of the following painters is famous for rendering the first secular painting, *Giovanni Arnolfini and His Wife?*

   A. Robert Campin
   B. Jan van Eyck
   C. Claus Suter
   D. Leonardo da Vinci

5. Which of the following artists painted the *Blonde Odalisque*?

   A. Jean-Antoine Watteau
   B. Jean-Honoré Fragonard
   C. Johann Baptist Zimmerman
   D. Frances Boucher

6. Which geographic location is considered the "cradle of civilization"?

   A. Greece
   B. Egypt
   C. Mesopotamia
   D. Babylon

7. The Church of St. Sophia, also known as the Hagia Sophia, is a prime example of

   A. Byzantine architecture.
   B. Early Christian architecture.
   C. Romanesque architecture.
   D. Gothic architecture.

8. The first book to be printed using moveable type was the

   A. *Gutenberg Bible.*
   B. *Nuremberg Chronicle.*
   C. *Four Horseman of the Apocalypse.*
   D. *Peace of Augsburg.*

9. *The Family of Charles IV is* a portrait by Francisco Goya that

   A. idealized patriotism.
   B. disguised his criticism.
   C. idealized the monarchy.
   D. celebrated family.

10. Stepped pyramids were built in Egypt during the period

   A. called the Early Dynastic Period.
   B. of the Old Kingdom.
   C. of the Middle Kingdom.
   D. of the New Kingdom.

11. Much of early Christian art can be found in

    A. basilicas.
    B. late-period Roman houses.
    C. abandoned temples.
    D. catacombs.

12. In which of the following frescoes did Leonardo da Vinci blend geometric balance and calm restraint with the contrast of chaos and emotion?

    A. *Virgin of the Rocks*
    B. *Creation of Adam*
    C. *The Last Supper*
    D. *Agnelo Doni*

13. A baldacchino (also known as a baldachin) is

    A. a massive canopy structure.
    B. a three-paneled painting, usually on wood.
    C. an orderly path between flowerbeds.
    D. a genre painting.

14. Which of the following painters is famous for rendering the *Oath of Horatii*?

    A. Anton Raphael Mengs
    B. Joshua Reynolds
    C. Jacques-Louis David
    D. Georges de La Tour

15. Which of the following works was created by Joseph Mallord William Turner?

    A. *Wanderer Above a Sea of Mist*
    B. *The Raft of Medusa*
    C. *Dutch Boats in a Gale*
    D. *The Fog Warning*

16. In Egyptian art, which artistic technique presented a profile or side view of people and animals?

    A. Hieratic scale
    B. Meander pattern
    C. Contrapposto
    D. Composite view

17. Although the Church of St. Sophia in Constantinople was known to be decorated with beautiful Byzantine mosaics, the best surviving examples can be found in which of the following churches?

A. Church of St. Michael
B. Church of San Vitale
C. Cathedral of Pisa
D. Modena Cathedral

18. Michelangelo's statue of the *Pietà* centered on a common theme in earlier art, depicting

A. the crucifixion of Jesus Christ.
B. the creation of Adam.
C. Mary holding her dead son Jesus.
D. the Old Testament David.

19. Which one of the following artists created *The Life of Harriet Tubman, No 4, 1939–1940*?

A. Grant Wood
B. Edward Hopper
C. Dorothea Langue
D. Jacob Lawrence

20. Which of the following is a well-preserved mortuary temple built for the first female ruler of Egypt?

A. Amun-Re
B. Hatshepsut's Temple
C. The Giza Necropolis
D. D. Nefertiti

21. Sculpted coffins are called

A. icons.
B. sarcophagi.
C. portals.
D. buttresses.

22. Which of the following artists created *Autumn Rhythm (Number 30)*?

A. Ellsworth Kelly
B. Jackson Pollock
C. Joseph Stella
D. Andy Warhol

23. Which of the following paintings best represents Fauvism?

    A. *The Old Guitarist*
    B. *The Woman with a Hat*
    C. *La Bouteille de Suze*
    D. *The Portuguese*

24. Which of the following artists painted *Rouen Cathedral, West Façade, Sunlight*?

    A. Pierre-August Renoir
    B. Claude Monet
    C. Edgar Degas
    D. Mary Cassatt

25. Which of the following painters painted himself into the portrait of *Las Meninas (The Maids of Honor)*?

    A. Diego Velàzquez
    B. Zurbaràn
    C. Carlo Maderno
    D. El Greco

26. What is the title of the altarpiece by Konrad Witz that is the earliest realistic depiction of landscape?

    A. *Mérode Altarpiece*
    B. *Miraculous Draft of Fishes*
    C. *Madonna of the Meadow*
    D. *Garden of Earthly Delights*

27. Which of the following art styles best represents the depiction of unfettered and irrational thought without adherence to any moral or aesthetic standards?

    A. Surrealism
    B. Cubism
    C. Expressionism
    D. Bauhaus

28. The *Temple of Apollo at Didyma* and the *Venus de Milo* are examples of which of the following styles?

A. Corinthian
B. Theatrical
C. Doric
D. Verism

29. Which of the following is the architectural feature that distinguished Romanesque and Gothic churches from those of the Byzantine and Early Christian periods?

A. Flying buttress
B. Pointed arch
C. Stained-glass window
D. Crossing square

30. *One and Three Chairs* by Joseph Kosuth is what type of art?

A. Minimalism
B. Pop Art
C. Hard-Edge Abstraction
D. Conceptual

31. Who is the architect responsible for building the Guggenheim Museum in Spain?

A. Jean-Michel Basquiat
B. Bill Voila
C. Frank Lloyd Wright
D. Frank Gehry

32. The Rococo architectural style emphasizes

A. asymmetry.
B. symmetry.
C. republican liberty.
D. simplicity and grace.

33. Vincent van Gogh painted *Starry Night* using thick applications of paint called

A. synthetism.
B. impressionism.
C. impasto.
D. *en plein air.*

34. During which period did the Greeks create many stone sculptures of life-size male nudes?

    A. Classical
    B. Archaic
    C. Hellenistic
    D. Geometric

35. Painting on vellum is called

    A. illumination.
    B. fresco.
    C. iconography.
    D. encaustic painting.

36. Which of the following sixteenth-century artists painted *The Triumph of Death*?

    A. Hieronymus Bosch
    B. Peter Bruegel the Eder
    C. Albrecht Altdorfer
    D. Hans Holbein the Younger

37. Which of the following artworks is an expression of feminism?

    A. *Woman I*
    B. *The Dinner Party*
    C. *Bed*
    D. *Shot Marilyns*

38. Which of the following architects designed the US Capitol Building?

    A. Charles Bulfinch
    B. Thomas Jefferson
    C. Christopher Wren
    D. William Kent

39. Contemporary Art is best described by which of the following terms?

    A. Existentialism
    B. Abstraction
    C. Neo-Expressionism
    D. Pluralism

40. During the Early Roman Empire, a new form of idealism was expressed in art and architecture, exemplified in which of the following statues?

A. *She-Wolf*
B. *Portrait of the Four Tetrarchs*
C. *Augustus of Prima Porta*
D. *Kritios Boy*

41. Which of the following techniques is also called a *one-point perspective*, with all lines converging to a single point in the distance?

A. Chiaroscuro
B. Illumination
C. Trompe l'oeil
D. Linear perspective

42. Which of the following artists is regarded as the precursor of Expressionism and Cubism?

A. Hieronymus Bosch
B. Jean Clouet
C. El Greco
D. Matthias Grünewald

43. Which of the following works was created by Antonio Canova?

A. *Cornelia Pointing to Her Children as Her Treasures*
B. *La Grande Odalisque*
C. *Psyche Revived by Cupid's Kiss*
D. *Bust of Benjamin Franklin*

44. The Arch of Constantine is best noted for its use of decorations from previously constructed monuments. Which of the following terms identifies the remnants?

A. Orders
B. Capitals
C. Spolia
D. Stelai

45. The doors dubbed by Michelangelo as "The Gates of Paradise" are made of

    A. bronze.
    B. marble.
    C. ceramic.
    D. wood.

46. Which work of art by Rodin made a symbolic statement?

    A. *Mahana No Atua*
    B. *The Thinker*
    C. *The Streetwalker*
    D. *The Child's Bath*

47. Which of the following artists painted *Luncheon on the Grass*?

    A. Théodore Géricault
    B. Thomas Cole
    C. Honoré Daumier
    D. Edward Manet

48. In which of the following frescoes did Diego Rivera emphasize the heroism and triumph of the Mexican Revolution?

    A. *Diego in My Thoughts*
    B. *The Persistence of Memory*
    C. *Distributing Arms*
    D. *The Old Guitarist*

49. Which of the following works uses video and audio as its media?

    A. *Horn Players*
    B. *The Crossing*
    C. *The Prevalence of Ritual: Baptism*
    D. *Dinner Party*

50. Which of the following artists is said to have paved the way for the later styles of Fauvism, Cubism, and Expressionism?

    A. Berthe Morisot
    B. Claude Monet
    C. Pierre-August Renoir
    D. Paul Cézanne

51. In general, art from the early twentieth century mostly focused on the

    A. pain and isolation of the modern world.
    B. a complete departure from nature.
    C. unique perceptions of the artist.
    D. the unconscious mind.

52. Which one of the following artists painted *The Birth of Venus*?

    A. Donatello
    B. Masaccio
    C. Leonardo da Vinci
    D. Botticelli

53. A piece of art combining various preexisting materials is called

    A. figurative art.
    B. an abstraction.
    C. a trompe l'oeil.
    D. a collage.

54. Thomas Eakins painted which of the following images of American life?

    A. *Max Schmitt in a Single Scull*
    B. *Snap the Whip*
    C. *The Fog Warning*
    D. *Breezing Up*

55. The *Spiral Jetty* is an example of

    A. combine painting.
    B. color stain painting.
    C. hard-edge abstraction.
    D. earthworks.

56. Which of the following churches represents the Romanesque style?

    A. Westminster Abbey
    B. Notre Dame
    C. Church of Saint Vincent
    D. Benedictine Abbey of Saint-Denis

57. Which of the following paintings by Rembrandt features a group capturing a moment in time?

A. *Bathsheba with King David's Letter*
B. *The Hundred Guilder Print*
C. *The Night Watch*
D. *Charles I at the Hunt*

58. Marcel Duchamp was a champion of which of the following art movements?

A. De Stijl
B. Dada
C. Surrealism
D. Social Realism

59. Which of the following artists was a controversial figure and famous for his use of tenebrism?

A. Gian Lorenzo Bernini
B. Francesco Borromini
C. Giovanni Battista Gaulli
D. Michelangelo Merisi

60. The technique of depicting a person from behind viewing a scene is known as

A. empiricism.
B. rückenfigur.
C. chiaroscuro.
D. tenebrism.

ANSWER KEY AND EXPLANATIONS

1. C	13. A	25. A	37. B	49. B
2. C	14. C	26. B	38. A	50. D
3. D	15. C	27. A	39. D	51. C
4. B	16. D	28. B	40. C	52. D
5. D	17. B	29. D	41. D	53. D
6. C	18. C	30. D	42. C	54. A
7. A	19. D	31. D	43. C	55. D
8. A	20. B	32. A	44. C	56. C
9. B	21. B	33. C	45. A	57. C
10. A	22. B	34. B	46. B	58. B
11. D	23. B	35. A	47. D	59. D
12. C	24. B	36. B	48. C	60. B

1. **The correct answer is C.** Nicholas Poussin painted *The Rape of the Sabine Women*. Peter Paul Rubens (choice A) was the Flemish painter who painted *The Rape of the Daughters of Leucippus*. Anthony Van Dyck (choice B) is mostly known for his sympathetic portraiture. George de La Tour (choice D) was heavily influenced by Caravaggio and is known for his painting, *The Penitent Magdalene*.

2. **The correct answer is C.** Ziggurats are stepped towers upon which Sumerians built temples. An upright marker stone (choice A) is a stele. Stepped pyramids (choice B) were built in Egypt, whereas ziggurats were built in Mesopotamia. An amphitheater (choice D) is an open circular or oval building for spectators of dramatic or sporting events.

3. **The correct answer is D.** The Gothic style first developed in France during the middle of the twelfth century. Germany (choice A), Italy (choice B), and England (choice C) display Gothic architecture that was developed later on.

4. **The correct answer is B.** Flemish painter Jan van Eyck created the first known secular painting of the Renaissance. Robert Campin (choice A) was another Flemish painter known for emphasizing symbolism. Claus Suter (choice C) oversaw the construction of the Well of Moses. Leonardo da Vinci (choice D) painted his *Mona Lisa* later, in the sixteenth century.

5. The correct answer is D. William Boucher painted the suggestive and controversial *Blonde Odalisque*. Jean-Antoine Watteau (choice A) was famous for his *Pilgrimage to Cythera*. Johann Baptist Zimmerman (choice B) is considered one of the last French Rococo painters, and he is best known for *The Swing*. Johann Baptist Zimmerman (choice C) painted the ceiling of Wieskirche in Bavaria.

6. The correct answer is C. Mesopotamia is known as the "cradle of civilization." Greece (choice A) and Egypt (choice B) were early civilizations created after Mesopotamia. Babylon (choice D) is a city in Mesopotamia that developed after the Sumerian and Akkadian cultures.

7. The correct answer is A. The Church of St. Sophia in Constantinople, which combines the longitudinal shape of a Roman basilica with a domed central plan, represents the Byzantine style. Early Christian architecture (choice B) closely followed classical Roman style. Romanesque architecture (choice C) was influenced by a number of styles, not just Roman. Gothic architecture (choice D) developed later on in the Middle Ages.

8. The correct answer is A. The *Gutenberg Bible* was the first book to be printed using moveable type. The *Nuremberg Chronicle* (choice B) was published later. *The Four Horseman of the Apocalypse* (choice C) is a woodcut illustration found in a publication by Albrecht Dürer. The *Peace of Augsburg* (choice D) was a document that recorded the compromise ending wars in Northern Europe.

9. The correct answer is B. Although the formal portrait of the Spanish royal family is painted in a lavish style that highlights the family's wealth and power, it is a veiled criticism of their arrogance and vanity. Goya supported citizens who stood up for their country (choice A) in his painting *The Third of May*. Rather than idealize the monarch (choice C) and his family (choice D), Goya expressed his disdain for the emptiness of court life.

10. **The correct answer is A.** Stepped pyramids were the earliest form of pyramids built during the Early Dynastic Period. The Old Kingdom (choice B), Middle Kingdom (choice C), and New Kingdom (choice D) followed the Early Dynastic Period.

11. **The correct answer is D.** The earliest Christian art is evident in the catacombs, underground burial chambers that were accessible to all Roman citizens. Basilicas (choice A) were created after Christianity became the dominant religion. Although Roman houses (choice B) were sometimes used as places of worship, the most enduring art is found in the catacombs. Christians avoided using temples (choice C), as they represented paganism and were meant to house the gods, not worshippers.

12. **The correct answer is C.** In *The Last Supper*, Leonardo combined a sense of geometric balance by placing the serene Jesus at the center of the composition flanked by the bewildered apostles. The *Virgin of the Rocks* (choice A) is a painted altarpiece by Leonardo da Vinci that emphasized grace and restraint. The *Creation of Adam* (choice B) is a fresco by Michelangelo that appears on the ceiling of the Sistine Chapel. *Agnelo Doni* (choice D) is a portrait by Raphael.

13. **The correct answer is A.** A baldacchino is a massive canopy structure, such as the one that was built over St. Peter's tomb in Rome. A three-paneled painting (choice B) is called a triptych. An orderly path between flowerbeds (choice C) is a parterre. A genre painting (choice D) is a scene about everyday people and the natural world.

14. **The correct answer is C.** Jacques-Louis David painted the *Oath of Horatii*. Anton Raphael Mengs (choice A) painted the ceiling fresco *Parnassus*. Joshua Reynolds (choice B) painted *Lady Sarah Bunbury Sacrificing to the Graces*. Georges de La Tour (choice D) was heavily influenced by Caravaggio and is known for his painting, *The Penitent Magdalen*.

15. **The correct answer is C.** *Dutch Boats in a Gale* was painted by Turner. *Wanderer Above a Sea of Mist* (choice A) is a painting by Caspar David Friedrich. *The Raft of Medusa* (choice B) is a painting by Théodore Géricault. *The Fog Warning* (choice D) was painted by Winslow Homer.

16. **The correct answer is D.** The composite view presented a profile or side view of animals. Hieratical scale (choice A) refers to using relative size to reflect importance. The meander pattern (choice B) is a geometric design used in Greek pottery. Contrapposto (choice C) is a sculptural style that emphasizes human movement.

17. **The correct answer is B.** The Church of San Vitale in Ravenna, which was built at the same time as the Church of St. Sophia, survives as a prime example of Byzantine mosaics. The Church of St. Michael (choice A), the Cathedral of Pisa (choice C), and the Modena Cathedral (choice D) are indicative of the Romanesque style.

18. **The correct answer is C.** Michelangelo's *Pietà* depicts Mary holding her dead son Jesus in her lap as she mourns. Christ's crucifixion (choice A) is a common theme in religious art, but not the actual subject of the *Pietà*. The creation of Adam (choice B) is depicted in Michelangelo's painting in the Sistine Chapel. The Old Testament David (choice D) is also a common theme in sculpture, but he was not the subject portrayed in the *Pieta*.

19. **The correct answer is D.** Jacob Lawrence painted *The Life of Harriet Tubman, No 4, 1939–1940*. Grant Wood (choice A) and Edward Hopper (choice B) are best known for their stark depictions of American life. Dorothea Lange (choice C) was a photographer who captured the destitution of migrant farmers in California.

20. **The correct answer is B.** Hatshepsut's Deir el-Bahri Temple is a well-preserved mortuary temple built for the first female ruler whose name has been recorded. Amun-Re (choice A) is another Egyptian temple located at Karnak. The Giza Necropolis (choice C) is where the Great Sphinx and Pyramids of Giza are found. Nefertiti (choice D) was Akhenaten's queen.

21. **The correct answer is B.** Sarcophagi are sculpted coffins that are placed in burial locations. Icons (choice A) are paintings of religious figures or scenes on wooden panels. Portals (choice C) are church entryways adorned with semicircular arches. Buttresses (choice D) are architectural supports for high ceilings.

22. **The correct answer is B.** Jackson Pollock painted *Autumn Rhythm (Number 30)*. Ellsworth Kelly (choice A) is known for his *Red, Blue, and Green* piece. Joseph Stella (choice C) is famous for his *Mas o Menos*. Andy Warhol (choice D) is best known for his *32 Campbell Soup Cans*, *Green Coca-Cola Bottles*, and *Shot Marilyns*.

23. **The correct answer is B.** *The Woman with a Hat* by Henri Matisse best represents Fauvism. *The Old Guitarist* (choice A) best represents Picasso's Blue Period and the beginnings of Cubism, while *La Bouteille de Suze* (choice C) is an example of Picasso's Synthetic Cubism. *The Portuguese* (choice D) by Braque best represents Analytic Cubism.

24. **The correct answer is B.** Claude Monet painted *Rouen Cathedral, West Façade, Sunlight*, which is one of his most notable works. Pierre-August Renoir (choice A) is best known for his scenes of Parisian life, such as *Le Moulin de La Galette*. Edgar Degas (choice C) was fascinated with movement, as shown in his painting *The Rehearsal*. Marie Cassatt (choice C) is best known for her mother-and-child scenes.

25. **The correct answer is A.** In *Las Meninas (The Maids of Honor)*, Velàzquez is present in the painting, standing at his easel. Zurbaràn (choice B), who devoted himself to the expression of religion and faith, painted *The Birth of the Virgin*. Carlo Maderno (choice C) oversaw the first Baroque additions to St. Peter's in Rome. El Greco (choice D) painted during the Spanish Renaissance and is regarded as the precursor of Expressionism and Cubism.

26. **The correct answer is B.** The *Miraculous Draft of Fishes* has been noted as the earliest realistic depiction of landscape based on an artist's personal observation. The *Mérode Altarpiece* (choice A) is a three-panel painting by Robert Campin. The *Madonna of the Meadow* (choice C) is a painting by Raphael. *The Garden of Earthly Delights* (choice D) is a triptych by Hieronymus Bosch.

27. **The correct answer is A.** As defined by the movement's manifesto, surrealism reflected unfettered thought, irrational and outside of any moral or aesthetic standards. Cubism (choice B) emphasized intellectual analysis. Expressionism (choice C) highlighted the innermost, turbulent emotions of an artist. The Bauhaus School (choice D) was dedicated to blending the fine and applied arts using manufacturing to create practical, everyday products, such as chairs and textiles.

28. **The correct answer is B.** *Theatricality* is the term identifying an artistic movement that is exemplified by the *Temple of Apollo at Didyma* and the *Venus de Milo.* Corinthian (choice A) and Doric (choice C) refer to architectural column styles. Verism (choice D) is a sculptural style that emphasizes reproducing an exact likeness of a subject.

29. **The correct answer is D.** The crossing square is the architectural feature that best distinguishes the Romanesque and Gothic churches from earlier churches in classic Roman or Byzantine styles. The flying buttress (choice A), pointed arch (choice B), and stained-glass window (choice C) are all examples of the Gothic style.

30. **The correct answer is D.** *One and Three Chairs* is an example of Conceptual Art. Minimalism (choice A) is best exemplified by repeated basic lines and the use of one color, such as in *Mas o Menos.* Pop Art (choice B) was created by artists Andy Warhol and Roy Lichtenstein. Hard-Edge Abstraction (choice C) is best exemplified by the painting *Red, Blue, and Green.*

31. **The correct answer is D.** The Guggenheim Museum in Bilbao, Spain, was built by Frank Gehry. Jean-Michel Basquiat (choice A) was an artist who focused on politics and racial identity. Bill Viola (choice B) is a video artist. Frank Lloyd Wright (choice C) designed the Guggenheim Museum in New York City.

32. **The correct answer is A.** The Rococo style emphasizes asymmetry and elaborate ornamentation. Symmetry (choice B), republican liberty (choice C), and simplicity and grace (choice D) are all hallmarks of Neoclassicism.

33. **The correct answer is C.** Vincent van Gogh used an impasto technique to paint *Starry Night*. Synthetism (choice A) was a term coined by Paul Gaugin to mean the synthesis of observation and impression. Impressionism (choice B) is a style of art that emphasizes an artist's impression of a scene rather than a close depiction. *En plein air* (choice D) means "in plain air" or "outdoors," where Impressionists preferred to paint to capture the effects of sunlight.

34. **The correct answer is B.** Many life-size stone sculptures of male nudes were created during the Archaic Period. Classical (choice A), Hellenistic (choice C), and Geometric (choice D) are other periods of Greek history and art.

35. **The correct answer is A.** The technique that artists used to paint Gospel manuscripts on vellum is called illumination. A fresco (choice B) is painting technique applied to fresh plaster. Iconography (choice C) is the interpretation of artistic images. Encaustic painting (choice D) is a method of painting on wood panels using heated wax.

36. **The correct answer is B.** Peter Bruegel the Elder painted *The Triumph of Death*. Hieronymus Bosch (choice A) painted the *Garden of Earthly Delights*. Albert Altdorfer (choice C) was an artist from Germany who focused more on painting landscape elements. Hans Holbein the Younger (choice D) painted a wedding portrait of *King Henry VIII* in 1540.

37. The correct answer is B. *The Dinner Party* celebrates historically significant women and their accomplishments. *Woman I* (choice A) Willem de Kooning painting that depicts a woman who appears to be snarling. *Bed* (choice C) is a combine painting that joins paint and pencil with a pillow, sheet, and quilt on wood supports. *Shot Marilyns* (choice D) are a series of Pop Art portraits of Marilyn Monroe.

38. The correct answer is A. Charles Bulfinch designed the US Capitol Building. Thomas Jefferson (choice B) designed Monticello. Christopher Wren (choice C) was responsible for renovating St. Paul's Cathedral. William Kent (choice D) designed Chiswick House.

39. The correct answer is D. Pluralism, the notion of a limitless variety of styles and media, best describes Contemporary Art. Existentialism (choice A) may be one of the ideas expressed, but not the only idea expressed in today's art. Abstraction (choice B) and Neo-Expressionism (choice C) are just two styles of art in existence today.

40. The correct answer is C. The first Roman emperor, Augustus, commissioned *Augustus of Prima Porta* to portray his idealized self for posterity. *She-Wolf* (choice A) is a bronze statue from Etruscan times. The *Portrait of the Four Tetrarchs* (choice B) is from a later period. *Kritios Boy* (choice D) is a statue from the Greek classical period.

41. The correct answer is D. The linear perspective helped artists create a three-dimensional illusion on a two-dimensional surface. Chiaroscuro (choice A) is the use of light and shadow to create a sense of depth. Illumination (choice B) is the illustration of written text on vellum. Trompe l'oeil (choice C) is a painted illusion of a three-dimensional object.

42. The correct answer is C. El Greco is regarded as the precursor of Expressionism and Cubism because of his highly dramatic and expressive style, his distortion of proportions, and stressing of imagination and intuition. Hieronymus Bosch (choice A) was known for his fantastic imagery in the *Garden of Earthly Delights*. Jean Clouet (choice B) was an official portrait painter for the French court. Matthias Grünewald (choice D) focused on religious themes using exaggerated realism and numerous details.

43. The correct answer is C. *Psyche Revived by Cupid's Kiss* is Canova's most respected sculpture. *Cornelia Pointing to Her Children as Her Treasures* (choice A) is an Angelika Kauffman painting. *La Grande Odalisque* (choice B) is a painting by Ingres. *The Bust of Benjamin Franklin* (choice D) was sculpted by Jean-Antoine Houdon.

44. The correct answer is C. Spolia is the term used to identify the use of decorations from previously constructed monuments. Orders (choice A) are styles of architecture. Capitals (choice B) are the tops of architectural columns. Stelai (choice D) are stone slabs that are inscribed, carved, or painted with imagery.

45. The correct answer is A. Ghiberti was commissioned to create the set of bronze doors called "The Gates of Paradise." Marble (choice B) and ceramic (choice C) were mostly used to fashion figures. Wood (choice D) was used for many artistic works in Northern Europe, but not for these doors.

46. The correct answer is B. *The Thinker* is a sculpture by Rodin that symbolized human despair. *Mahana No Atua* (choice A) is a painting by Gaugin that blended actual and symbolic detail. *The Streetwalker* (choice C) is a painting by Henri de Toulouse-Lautrec. *The Child's Bath* (choice D) is a painting by Mary Cassatt.

47. The correct answer is D. Edward Manet painted *Luncheon on the Grass*, which scandalized many of his contemporaries. Théodore Géricault (choice A) was famous for his dramatic *Raft of Medusa*. Thomas Cole (choice B) brought Romanticism to the United States with his painting *The Oxbow*. Honoré Daumier (choice C) created *Le Ventre Legislatif* to criticize the French government.

48. The correct answer is C. Diego's *Distributing Arms* was executed in what he believed to be an ancient Mayan technique, and it emphasized the heroism and triumph of the Mexican Revolution. *Diego in My Thoughts* (choice A) was painted by Mexican artist Frida Kahlo and highlighted her fervent wish to survive and conquer death. The *Persistence of Memory* (choice B) is a surrealistic painting by Salvador Dali. *The Old Guitarist* (choice D) is a painting by Picasso.

49. The correct answer is B. *The Crossing* consists of two simultaneously presented videos with overwhelming sound effects. *Horn Players* (choice A) is a combination visual piece about African American jazz artists by Jean-Michel Basquiat. *The Prevalence of Ritual: Baptism* (choice C) is a Romare Bearden collage celebrating African American culture. *The Dinner Party* (choice D) celebrates historically significant women and their accomplishments.

50. The correct answer is D. Paul Cézanne's analytic, almost sculptural style paved the way for later styles. Berthe Morisot (choice A), Claude Monet (choice B), and Pierre-August Renoir (choice C) were all Impressionists who preferred a softer style of painting.

51. The correct answer is C. Most of the art from the modern world can be generalized as the unique perceptions of individual artists. Some modern artists focused on the pain and suffering in the world, but not all, so choice A is not the best answer. Choice B is also not the best answer because some modern art is realistic and not a complete departure from nature. Choice D can be eliminated because not all modern art is a reflection of the unconscious mind.

52. The correct answer is D. Botticelli painted *The Birth of Venus*. Donatello (choice A) was famous for his sculptures. Masaccio (choice B) painted the *Expulsion of Adam and Eve from Eden*. Leonardo da Vinci (choice C) was an artist from the sixteenth century best known for his *Mona Lisa* and *The Last Supper*.

53. **The correct answer is D.** A collage is a piece of art composed by combining preexisting materials. Figurative art (choice A) is representative art. An abstraction (choice B) is any work of art that is completely removed from the depiction of reality. A trompe l'oeil (choice C) is a painted illusion of a three-dimensional object.

54. **The correct answer is A.** Thomas Eakins painted *Max Schmitt in a Single Scull*. *Snap the Whip* (choice B), *The Fog Warning* (choice C), and *Breezing Up* (choice D) were all painted by Winslow Homer.

55. **The correct answer is D.** The *Spiral Jetty* is an example of earthworks and site-specific art. Combine painting (choice A) involves attaching everyday objects to a canvas. Color stain painting (choice B) is an abstract work created by pouring paint on a canvas. Hard-edge abstraction (choice C) consists of exact, smooth planes of color on canvas.

56. **The correct answer is C.** The Church of Saint Vincent in Spain is an early example of Romanesque architecture. Westminster Abbey (choice A), Notre Dame (choice B), and the Benedictine Abbey of Saint-Denis (choice D) all exemplify the Gothic style.

57. **The correct answer is C.** In *The Night Watch*, Rembrandt captures a military group in a dramatic moment in time. *Bathsheba with King David's Letter* (choice A) focuses on a main character. *The Hundred Guilder Print* (choice B) is an etching known for reflecting empathy and pathos. *Charles I at the Hunt* (choice D) is a portrait by Anthony Van Dyck.

58. **The correct answer is B.** Marcel Duchamp's famous Fountain, which is a urinal placed upside-down, is typical of the Dada movement. The artist best known for his De Stijl (choice A) compositions was Piet Mondrian. Salvador Dali and Joan Miro are the best-known Surrealistic artists (choice C). Social Realism (choice D) was represented by many different artists.

59. **The correct answer is D.** Michelangelo Merisi, also known as Caravaggio, was noted for his technique of tenebrism. Gian Lorenzo Bernini (choice A) designed the massive baldacchino over St. Peter's tomb. Francesco Borromini (choice B) is famous for designing the ceiling structure in the church of Sant'Ivo. Giovanni Battisti Gaulli (choice C) painted the ceiling of Il Gesu, the Jesuit mother church.

60. **The correct answer is B.** Rückenfigur is a composition device depicting a person from behind viewing the scene. Empiricism (choice A) is the observation of factual reality. Chiaroscuro (choice C) and tenebrism (choice D) are techniques that manipulate the lighting of a scene.

Like what you see? Peterson's offers access to color images, practice tests, instructional videos, flashcards, and more online at **www.petersons.com/ testprep/dsst.** Use coupon code **DSST2020** at checkout for **75% off the first month!** Offer expires July 1, 2021.

CPSIA information can be obtained
at www.ICGtesting.com
Printed in the USA
JSHW042125200722
28277JS00012B/140